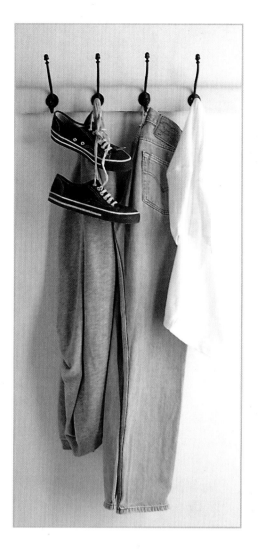

sewing classic
CLOTHES

RENÉ BERGH

sewing classic CLOTHES that fit

photography by ryno
illustrations by dave snook

BETTER
WAY
BOOKS

Cincinnati, Ohio

ACKNOWLEDGEMENTS

I would like to extend my sincere thanks to the publishing team at Struik: Linda de Villiers, Petal Palmer, Joy Clack and Bev Dodd for their hard work, understanding of the concept of this book and coming up with a superb design. Once again, Dave Snook has excelled himself with his beautiful illustrations, and I am extremely grateful to him. I also wish to thank Sylvie Hurford and Ryno for their professionalism, talent and skillful interpretation of this project, resulting in wonderful photographs. Siobhan O'Shea of Woolworths, Catherine Moore, Ruth at Polo Manufacturing, Juanita Pacheco, Xtra Shoes, Kamala Italian Imports, Sue and Paul McAdams of Loft Living and Smiley's Warehouse supplied us with clothes and accessories for photography and to them I would like to express my gratitude. Finally, a special thanks to my mother, Eunice Duffett for looking after my dog, and to my sons, Justin and Hayden for their encouragement and support.

RENÉ BERGH

First published in North America
in 2000 by Betterway Books
an imprint of F&W Publications, Inc.
1507 Dana Avenue
Cincinnati, OH 45207
1-800/289-0963

ISBN 1-55870-570-8

Editor: Joy Clack
Concept designer: Odette Marais
Designer: Beverley Dodd
Design coordinator: Petal Palmer
Photographer: Ryno
Stylist: Sylvie Hurford
Illustrator: Dave Snook
Proofreader and indexer: Brenda Brickman

10 9 8 7 6 5 4 3 2 1

Reproduction by Hirt & Carter Cape (Pty) Ltd
Printed and bound by Times Offset (M) Sdn Bhd

Contents

Introduction

A classic garment is an item your daughter borrows from your wardrobe and then refuses to return. Classic clothes embody everything that is stylish and elegant, with a design that is both timeless and fashionable, and where the colour, cloth and cut is of a high standard. This includes the modern classics such as jeans, the T-shirt and the denim jacket, all of which have become indispensable items in every woman's wardrobe.

Select your essential basics with care and ensure that the fit is perfectly compatible with your body's shape. The secret is simply this: understand your body, adjust and customize the patterns by pin-fitting them, and mix great tailoring with quality cloth. This is the key to classic dressing.

Classic ingredients

The three basic ingredients to successful classic dressing are colour, cloth and cut. The most workable wardrobe is based on a coordinated system where each item has a link in colour and shape to another garment. If you can successfully mix and match your wardrobe, you will find that the possibilities are endless.

Basic designs that are not cluttered with detail are more versatile and will, therefore, remain useful ingredients throughout several seasons. Learn to care for your garments to ensure a long life. Follow washing instructions, including those for all trimmings. Wear garments with care: hitch up trouser knees and straight skirts before sitting or bending, and, if necessary, have a protective coating applied to garments that are difficult or expensive to clean. Use padded hangers for items made from thin fabric, and shaped hangers for tailored garments. Combining these ingredients will guarantee a successful result.

Classic Ingredients

Colour is one of the most important aspects of classic dress. It can enhance your good features or accentuate the bad ones. Factors such as emotions, super-stitions, prejudice and insecurity govern the choice of colour. To develop a good sense of colour, experiment in front of the mirror and observe people's reactions towards different colours. This will build up confidence in your own judgement. Forget about the old-fashioned rules that presuppose the use of certain colours for different skin and hair types, and don't allow colour planning to become a habit by wearing only colours that are familiar and safe.

Classic colours never change. Black, navy, grey and beige and, to a lesser extent, burgundy, brown and bottle green are classic colours. On their own they may seem rather conservative, but they can easily be lifted with brighter accessories. Adopt a versatile approach and use a single, neutral colour as a backdrop for every-thing else, then build on from there with related and contrasting colours. Certain combinations are guaranteed to look striking, but beware of over-coordinating colour combinations. Instead, intro-duce an unexpected third colour and see the results.

Use pure white with caution – cream or off-white might be more appealing. Consider these pointers regarding the use of colour before completing your outfit.

These classic neutrals are versatile and can be worn successfully by most people.

Fabrics vary greatly in texture, weight and bulk. Be sure to select a quality that is appropriate to the style.

Cloth selection is crucial. Quality is an elusive factor that cannot be exclusively determined by the cost of the fabric. Learn to recognize it by touch. Feel the fabric's weight, bulk and texture. Is it crease-resistant, does it suit you, and is it appropriate for the garment's intended use? Is it washable? Consider all these aspects before purchasing your fabric, as inferior quality never justifies the time and effort spent on it.

Identifying fabric is not a simple task, as man-made fibres are constantly being modified and blended with others. Always check the labels for cloth composition.

This will also influence the washing instructions. Comfortable clothing is mainly determined by the fabric's ability to allow the evaporation of perspiration. Natural fibres, for example wool, cotton, silk and linen are popular because of their absorbent quality. To improve the absorbency of man-made fibres, some are crimped, while others are loosely woven to increase ventilation. Another factor relating to comfort is the degree of stretch in the fabric. Some fibres have natural elasticity, while others have elasticity in their structure. Man-made fibres produced from wood, coal and oil are usually less expensive, easier to

maintain, and hold their shape better than natural fibres. They also require little or no ironing and retain permanent pleats.

Textures used can vary from bouclés and corduroys to lace and satins, depending on the style of the garment. There are tweeds, Jacquards, prints and plains; slub, grosgrain, twill and taffeta; brocade, seersucker, net and organza ... There are also various finishes such as waterproofing, embossing, brushing and glazing, and fabrics can be treated to resist creases, stains, shrinkage and even fire. Consider all these factors before selecting your cloth.

11

Classic Ingredients

Cut, as it applies to fashion, is often used synonymously with fit and shape. The ability to relate detail and silhouette lines to one another in a flattering manner requires a basic understanding of the visual element of line. Eye movements are influenced by lines, which also establish shape and cut. The clever use of line can subtly draw attention to a particular area of a garment.

A classic garment can be defined as basic in design, versatile and relatively modest in appearance. A well-cut, classic garment should not be too tight, too revealing or extreme in any way. It should be comfortable and fit properly, and should not move about or need constant adjustment. Very often ready-made garments will need to be altered to correct their fit, or

patterns may need to be customized before sewing to adapt them to your body shape (see Adjusting and customizing patterns on page 40). A well-cut garment, which closely follows the natural line of the figure, is particularly revealing. Classic shapes like these have a permanent place in fashion and provide an invaluable starting point for designers.

Above: *A simple cowl neck is always elegant and softens the neckline with its gentle folds.*
Opposite: *The classic cut of these tailored jackets clearly follows the natural line of the body. They will always flatter the wearer.*

chapter two

Wardrobe planning

Your wardrobe should be seen as a family, where each item is related, some more closely than others. It should be based on logic and necessity, allowing a maximum number of options from the minimum number of clothes. Versatility is the key to a successful wardrobe. More scope for individuality can be derived from separates than from ready-made coordinates. The garments also need to be as timeless as possible to allow greater adaptation so that you can dress them up or down to suit the occasion. A single touch, such as a flash of colour, a piece of jewellery or a pair of brightly coloured sandals can transform the look and add an element of surprise.

There are classics in every type of dress, both modern and traditional. This is achieved by a clever combination of simple styling and quality cloth.

Modern Classics

Modern classics can be described as basic items of clothing that have become indispensable. The white T-shirt, for example, has become a classic shirt; blue denim jeans, the golf shirt, the tracksuit, the plain sweatshirt, the classic-cut denim jacket and the leather motorcycle jacket are all considered classics today. No wardrobe is complete without these items.

'I must confess it: in spite of the fact that some people think I am a man without vices, I am a T-shirt addict. It's the first thing that I put on in the morning and the last thing I take off at night!'

GEORGIO ARMANI

The T-shirt is an underrated basic. Plain white with a round or V-neck, this invaluable, neutral garment can take you through the day and night, providing it is not yellowing. During the day it c enhance jeans, shorts, skirts jackets, both sporty and tailore At night it can easily be dressed up with a striking piece of jewellery or silk trousers. The T-shirt also provides an extra layer of warmth in winte. worn under a V-neck sweater, for example. This year-round basic will not impose on your character, but will provide a canvas on which to create your own style.

The British Navy ordered sailors to sew sleeves into their sleeveless undershirts (vests) to screen their hairy armpits from royal view. In 1913 the United States Navy introduced a crew-necked, short-sleeved, white cotton undershirt to cover the chest hairs of sailors. Soon after, the rest of the armed forces adopted this garment. Its popularity also rose amongst labourers and, by the 1930s, large department stores in the United States began producing these undershirts to be worn as either inner or outer garments, thus giving birth to the T-shirt as it is known to us today.

Jeans rank as a classic only if the styling is minimal and functional, with double stitching on the seams, pockets and flies; reinforcements on pocket corners, the zip base and belt loops; a heavy-duty metal zip and at least five tough belt loops for a close fit at the waist. They need not necessarily be designer jeans, but they should fit well. Don't be fooled by tight jeans – they may appear to act like a corset, but after a couple of hours of wear your body heat will produce horizontal stress lines that emphasize any problem areas, such as hips or thighs. A loose, not baggy fit is best.

The strong twill-weave cotton fabric of white and blue threads originated from the French town of Nimes. During the 1850s Levi Strauss, a Bavarian, introduced denim jeans in San Francisco as workwear for goldminers. In 1872 these trousers were patented and, a year later, copper rivets at the stress points were included in the patent. Indigo-dyed denim jeans became fashionable in the 1950s in the USA and have never lost their popularity, thus giving jeans their status in the classic ranks.

The Golf Shirt is a preppy version of the basic T-shirt. Although it has been borrowed from the boys, it converts naturally to female wear. The traditional golf shirt is made in a knitted fine honeycomb/ waffle weave with a custom-made knitted collar and narrow cuffs on the short sleeves. The collar creates a slightly formal look. It has a short centre-front placket with three buttons. Very often a small logo is embroidered on the left-hand side or a pocket is present in its place.

In 1933, French tennis star René Lacoste, nicknamed 'Le Crocodile' launched a white, short-sleeved tennis shirt with a small crocodile emblem embroidered on the chest. Fred Perry, another Davis Cup winner, popularized a similar knitted tennis shirt. This style was also adopted by the golfing fraternity and is still worn by today's golfers.

The Tracksuit is not only confined to the fitness fanatic. It is a classic garment designed for comfort and warmth. A good quality tracksuit fabric – one that does not easily stretch or bag at the knees – is essential. To retain its shape, the ribbing should contain a percentage of Lycra (elastic thread). The most versatile style is a plain, round-necked sweatshirt with generous, cuffed pants. Both parts can be worn independently, for example the pants with a T-shirt and the sweatshirt with jeans. The tracksuit spells leisure and relaxation, but should not look sloppy.

The Sweatshirt is the modern version of the sweater. Emanating from the United States universities in the 1960s, it was adapted by Norma Kamali to its present status and has since become an essential classic, rapidly taking over from the knitted sweater. The easy wear and care characteristics of the sweat-shirt has added to its popularity. The fit may be loose or generous, depending on the application required, and the weight and construction of the fabric may vary, but the basic, classical shape consists of a ribbed crew neck, cuffs and hem band.

The classic denim jacket is an adaption from the original Eisenhower jacket, which was introduced during the Second World War. This jacket was named after the American Dwight Eisenhower, who was one of the key players in organizing the D-Day invasion of France. The denim jacket has been worn as casual wear by men and women alike since the mid-1940s.

The Leather Jacket with zips and studs originated from the back of a motorbike. Today, it has become the main ingredient of many a wardrobe. It is hard-wearing, water-proof, warm and comfortable and, what's more, it improves with age! This versatile jacket can look tough with jeans, delicate with lace, elegant with suitable accessories, and works as well with trousers as with skirts. The purchase of a leather jacket of capacious fit, neither too long nor cropped, preferably with generous sleeves, and in a practical colour, can result in a life-long investment.

The Denim Jacket simply does not date! The practical and class-less character of denim has made it into a utility classic. As with denim jeans, this jacket should be well constructed, with the necessary double stitching, reinforcements at strategic points and metal buttons down the front. Because of its classic cut, it looks as good on a woman as it does on a man. A generous fit, even one or two sizes bigger will allow more versatility. This jacket works well with soft and heavy fabrics alike and needn't only be worn with jeans. It is particularly handy during moderate weather.

Traditional Classics

Traditional classics can be described as fuss-free dressing without nostalgia. They consist of a jacket, skirt, trousers, shirt and, perhaps, a coat. Consider the simple modernity of the classic designer: Jean Muir's crepe jersey and the masterly reworking, season after season, of the little black dress. The 'British look' is a traditional classic style that shouldn't be defined as dull and stuffy, but rather as low-profile apparel.

'There is nothing more clean and classic than a white shirt.
It has a twisted elegance that is very seductive.'

HELMUT LANG

20

The Shirt buttons down the front, and has minimal detail except for a shoulder yoke and possibly a pocket on the left front. It should fit comfortably, and be neither too tight nor oversized, and should preferably be plain, or have stripes or a small dobby design. As an alternative, the two-piece collar may be buttoned down as are Ivy League shirts. Natural fibres such as cotton and linen crease easily, but the inclusion of a small percentage of polyester will ensure that the shirt remains crisp at all times. The blouse, a more feminine version of the shirt (at times with frills or gathers), can be worn to soften the look of an austere ensemble.

The shirt first emerged during the Renaissance and had long sleeves, side slits and was collarless. It was worn by men as an undergarment. Later, ruffles were added, and by the 1700s a detachable stiffened neckband appeared. In 1896, Brooks Brothers in the USA popularized the button-down shirt collars originally worn by polo players in England. This style was appropriated by women in the 1950s and is still popular today.

Trousers can be made to look as smart as a skirt, but the cut and fit are crucial for a successful result. The most useful and flattering shape is usually the simplest: a straight-legged trouser softened by two front pleats at the waist. Flannel, corduroy and poly/viscose are good fabrics for this timeless, versatile classic. Movement is less restricting and the wearer can be warm, comfortable and elegant at the same time. Trousers also have an added advantage in that they can be used to successfully conceal any scars or varicose veins you may have. Skintight trousers are uncomfortable and unflattering. They should only be worn by slim people and should be cut in stretch fabrics.

Trousers were first worn by the horse-riding peoples of the Steppes and were introduced to Europe by the Venetians in the 16th century. They were only accepted as informal wear in the early 1800s, but were more commonly worn after 1920. Chanel's 'yachting pants' or Oxford bags were made popular by Marlene Dietrich in the early 1930s, but were only acceptable worn by women in the 1960s when unisex fashions became vogue.

The Jacket is the coordinating link in separates dressing, giving unity without the uniformity of a matching suit. It should lift an outfit and not just be a top layer. Traditional tweeds as well as plain gabardines are suitable fabrics to use, as long as they are as versatile and neutral as possible. A well-tailored jacket should be softly structured and not awkward to wear. Avoid exaggerated collars and revers, large pockets, wide shoulders, contrast trims and, especially, cheap looking buttons (although these can be easily replaced). Whether single or double-breasted, the classic jacket serves a purpose all year round and can be comfortably worn both in- and outdoors.

In the early 1900s men wore a loose-fitting, lightweight sports jacket called a blazer, which was originally made from striped flannel. It was adopted by women in the 1920s and worn with skirts, shirts and ties. The naval blazer with gilt buttons soon became a fashion item and has retained its classic rank since the 1970s. The traditional length for a blazer is to the top of the thigh, but most schools include a slightly shorter version as part of their formal uniform.

The Skirt is an essential item in every woman's wardrobe. It has ousted the dress and paved the way for separate dressing. The shapes may vary, but the straight, tailored skirt is the most flattering style and never dates. A centre back vent or pleat can be added to facilitate comfort when walking or sitting. The use of crease-resistant fabric is essential, and lining the skirt will add body to the fabric and prevent bagging across the back. Pleated skirts and kilts are also considered traditional, and create a softer, sportier look. Skirt lengths may vary according to fashion trends, but the knee-length skirt is timeless.

The first 'skirt' consisted of a fur pelt tied around the waist and was worn in Ethiopia about three million years ago by Lucy, the *Australopithecus*. Ancient sculptures dating back to 2500 BC showed Sumerian men and women wearing apron-like goat-skin skirts. Animal pelts were later replaced by cloth. During the Middle Ages the skirt succeeded the tunic and has remained a garment worn by women since then. Although the kilt was worn before the Middle Ages, it only became identified with Scotland in the 17th century. It was promoted by Queen Victoria and Prince Albert and has been fashionable since the 1940s in either tartan or plain.

The Little Black Dress is an item that no woman should be without. It can be worn during the day with modest adornment or dressed up for the evening simply by switching to more elaborate accessories. Its beauty lies in its simplicity. It always looks right and is best cut into a slim, sleek shape using a luxurious fabric such as crepe, silk or velvet. Deep navy, dark charcoal or even a deep red or bottle green will suffice if black is unsuitable. The dress may be sleeveless or long sleeved; high-necked or décolleté. The styling details are irrelevant, providing the overall design remains unpretentious and the original concept is not forgotten.

The little black dress emerged in the 1920s and was based on the lines of the chemise. It became the mainstay of all women attending the cocktail hour and an indispensable ingredient of every woman's wardrobe. In the 1920s and 1930s, Chanel and Molyneux popularized this enduring fashion item and it has since always been fashionable at some point in every decade.

The Coat is not as popular in the South as it is in the Northern hemisphere, mainly due to climatic conditions. The most substantial outlay in a wardrobe is a coat and it should, therefore, be classic. But a winter coat is not essential, a good raincoat will often suffice. It can be seasonless, complementing both summer and winter wardrobes. Burberry trench coats and single-breasted macs are sensible styles that won't date. The fit should be sufficiently generous to allow for extra layers of clothing underneath. Pockets are essential and detachable hoods very practical.

Historically, cloaks preceded coats and the redingote, or riding coat, only became popular in England in the 1720s. It was adopted by women by 1785 and developed into the modern coat over the years. The raglan – a coat with sleeves that continue to the collar instead of having armhole seams – was named after Field Marshal Lord Raglan in the late 1700s. This comfortable style remains fashionable to this day. In 1909 Thomas Burberry registered his waterproof gabardine raincoat with raglan sleeves. The style of this trench coat, known as a 'Burberry', has been copied worldwide.

Personal touch

Many women do not have an average figure outline so it is important to analyze your figure and develop an eye for selecting the styles that are best suited to your body's shape. Be sincere and objective, bearing in mind that no one is perfect and that classic dressing works for all shapes and sizes. Chart all your measurements accurately and take note of your posture.

Fitting is learning how to adjust and customize ready-made patterns by applying your measurements to them. It involves judgement, taste, understanding, and achieving a feeling of self-confidence, where you know that your clothes are not only comfortable but attractive. All garments need to be well-fitted so that when they are oversized, they appear fashionably loose-fitting, and when they are close-fitting they will still allow freedom of movement without being restrictive.

Fit

This may vary with fashion trends, but classic clothes seldom do. Traditional classics and jeans follow the natural body shape, allowing minimum ease: 5 cm (2 in) at the bust; 2.5 cm (1 in) at the waist; and 7.5 cm (3 in) at the hip. These patterns require precise fitting at the shoulders, bust, waist and hips, as well as sleeve and hem lengths. On trousers, the critical areas are the crotch seam and thigh area.

The fit of modern classics (the T-shirt, sweatshirt, tracksuit and denim jacket) tends to be more relaxed and requires less precision than the traditional fit. Here, the important checkpoints are the shoulders, which should follow the natural shoulder line, and the neckline, which should rest smoothly against the neck without gaping.

Fit checklist

Neckline to rest smoothly on collarbone. Collars can be buttoned comfortably.

Shoulder Seams to be straight across top of shoulder, ending at top of arm for set-in sleeves or sleeveless styles.

Sleeve Caps curve smoothly around armholes. Elbow dart or eased area falls at the elbow when arm is slightly bent. Sleeve should bend slightly forward below elbow.

Sleeve Hems or cuffs of shirt or dress to end at wristbones when arms are slightly bent. Jacket sleeves: allow 6–12 mm (¼–½ in) of shirt sleeves to show. Coat sleeves: end 6–12 mm (¼–½ in) below wristbones to cover shirt or dress sleeves.

Bust Shaping to fall at fullest part of bust and follow bust contours. Bust darts to end 2.5–5 cm (1–2 in) from bust point, depending on size of bust.

Bodice Back to fit smoothly, with darts or seams conforming to figure contours at shoulder blades and natural waist.

Waistline Seam, lower edge of waistband or waist shaping to fall at natural waist. Waistbands of skirts or trousers to allow a thumb's ease between waistband and abdomen.

Back Darts to end 12 mm–2.5 cm (½–1 in) short of fullest part of buttocks. Ease allows you to bend or sit without straining seams.

Buttocks and crotch seam to follow body contours. Darts to shape to contours without wrinkles, pulls or dimples. Jacket hem to fall above or below fullest part of buttocks.

Hemline to be equidistant from floor. Avoid placing hem at fullest part of calves or thighs. Hem on trousers to touch top of shoe heel.

Figure Analysis

To understand the difference between the average figure used to standardize commercial patterns and your own figure, you will need to analyze it. This will enable you to correctly adjust the fit and select flattering pattern styles. Look at yourself realistically and be objective as you compare your figure with the pattern averages. Focus on highlighting your good points, but bear in mind that most people do have areas that require camouflaging. In time, body shapes change, and it is important not to dwell on how you used to look, but concentrate on how you look right now.

By tracing a silhouette of your body, you will be able to analyze your figure objectively and more honestly than looking in the mirror. Ask a friend to help you. Remember that this outline will not be a perfect replica of your figure, but will disclose your general body shape, providing length proportions and figure contour guidelines.

What you will need:
- Large piece of paper
- Pencil or pen
- Ruler

What you should wear:
- Underwear or leotard
- No shoes
- Cord tied around the waist
- Short necklace around the neck

1 Draw a line lengthwise through the centre of the paper. Attach the paper to a smooth wall or door and stand centred against this line. Stand normally, with your shoulders and arms relaxed, chin up and heels against the wall or door. Your helper can now draw your outline, keeping the pen straight and parallel to the floor.

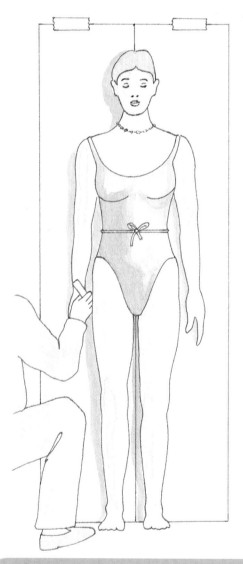

The end of the shoulder is at the shoulder joint and can be determined by raising the arm and feeling the indentation at the socket.

2 Before stepping away from the paper, mark the top of the head, the left and right sides of the base of the neck where the necklace rests, the ends of the shoulders, the under-arms at the creases, the waist where the cord is tied, the fullest part of the hips, and at the centre of the knees, as illustrated.

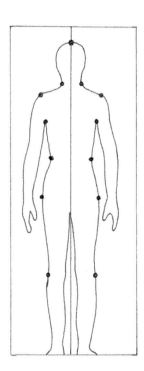

3 Draw a line at the top of the head, perpendicular to the centre line. Then draw lines connecting the various points, as illustrated. These lines will indicate your length proportions.

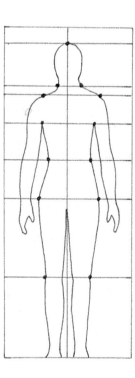

4 Remove the paper from the wall and fold it in half, matching the top of the head to the bottom of the paper. Fold it in half again and crease the folds. Match the underarm to the hipline and crease again. These crease lines will show the average length proportions for the hips, waist and knees.

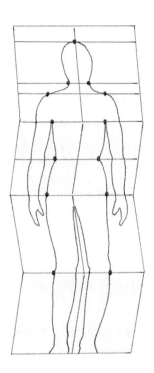

5 Join the shoulder and hip marks on both sides to indicate your body shape. You will now be able to see your outline as an abstract shape and can begin to analyze your figure objectively.

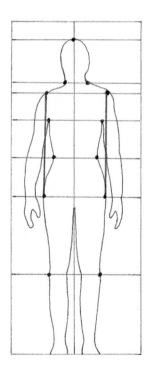

Length Proportions

On the average body, the length proportions are as follows: the hips are halfway between the top of the head and the floor; the waist is halfway between the the underarm and the hips; and the knees are halfway between the hips and the floor. Compare the creases of your outline to the average body outline to ascertain your true length proportions.

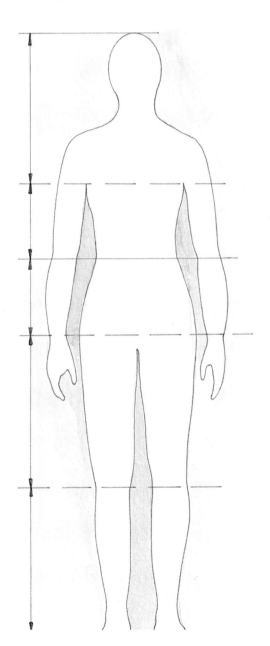

Body Shape

This can be catagorized into four main silhouettes. Check your outline to establish your shape.

*Shoulders and hips equally wide with a
clearly narrower waist.*

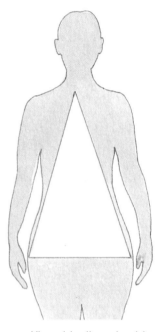

Hips wider than shoulders

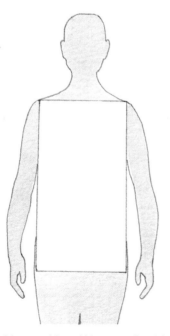

Shoulders, waist and hips equally wide.

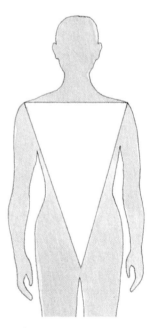

Shoulders wider than hips.

Shoulder Contours

These may be average, sloping or square. Sloping shoulders are usually also narrow, whereas square shoulders are normally wide. The average slope is 5 cm (2 in) from the neck-base line to the shoulder line. Measure the distance on your outline to determine the slope of your shoulders.

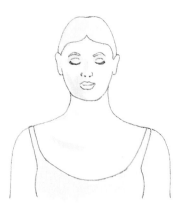

Arm Contours

The contours and lengths vary from person to person. Average arms are gently curved above and below the elbow; full arms are more heavily curved; and thin arms look quite bony with minimal muscular curves. The average wrist falls in line with the hips.

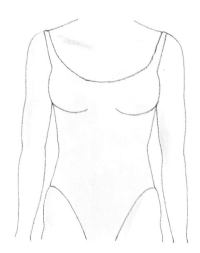

Waist and Hip Contours

The waist can be clearly verified using your outline drawing. The average waist is about 24-25.5 cm (9½-10 in) narrower than the hips; a thick waist is considerably less than that with little waist indentation; and a small waist much more than that with a pronounced indentation.

The hip contours can also be readily ascertained. The average hips are 18-23 cm (7-9 in) below the waist and 24-25.5 cm (9½-10 in) wider than the waist. Full hips are considerably larger than that and small hips considerably smaller than that.

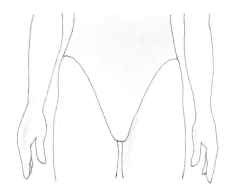

Thigh Contours

On the average body, the contours are softly rounded, with the inner thighs barely touching. Full thighs bulge on the outer and inner leg even when the feet are apart. Thin thighs look straight on the inner leg with a considerable space between the inner thighs.

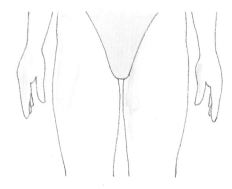

Body Profile

An outline of your profile will help to analyze your bust, abdomen and buttocks objectively. This can be done by photographing or tracing an outline of your body profile with the help of a friend. It is only necessary to outline from the neck to the mid-thigh, marking both the front and back edges.

Bust Profile

This is more accurate when wearing a well-fitted bra. Contours will alter according to the type of bra worn. The average bust will be a B-cup, softly rounded; a full bust, generously curved, will be a C-cup or larger; and a small bust with little or no curve, will be about an A-cup.

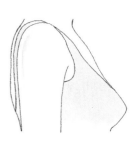

Abdomen Profile

The average abdomen is slightly rounded below the waist; the full abdomen curves prominently; and the flat abdomen runs straight below the waist, looking almost hollow. This profile can change with weight loss or gain.

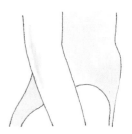

Buttocks Profile

Average buttocks have a small, high curve; full buttocks have a generous, rounded curve; flat buttocks have almost no curve; and swaybacked buttocks jut out from the hollow just below the waist. This profile is also affected by maturity, diet and muscle tone.

Detail	Flattering	Unflattering	Pattern Adjustments
LONG-WAISTED	Wide, high-rise waistbands; raised waistlines; short jackets; relaxed fit above waist.	Hip yokes; dropped waist-lines; snug fit above waist.	Lengthen bodice; lengthen crotch; shorten finished garment.
SHORT-WAISTED	Narrow waistbands; hip yokes; dropped waistlines; long jackets; blousing at or below waist.	Wide waistbands; patch pockets; short jackets.	Shorten bodice; raise hipline; lengthen finished garment.
SLOPING SHOULDERS	Cap, set-in and gathered sleeves; extended, padded shoulders; shoulder yokes.	Raglan, dolman, kimono and puffed sleeves; sleeveless and strapless styles; dropped shoulders.	Increase shoulder slope by adding shoulder pads to the regular slope shoulder pattern.
SQUARE SHOULDERS	Raglan, set-in, kimono and dolman sleeves; halter-necks; dropped shoulders.	Extended, padded shoulders; cap sleeve.	Decrease shoulder slope; omit shoulder pads when these are suggested in the pattern.
FULL ARMS	Long set-in sleeves, puffed sleeves, softly bloused sleeves.	Cap and fitted sleeves; sleeveless, halter-neck and strapless styles.	Increase upper arm on fitted and set-in sleeves.
THIN ARMS	Dolman, kimono, roll-up, elbow-length and short sleeves; full puffed and softly bloused sleeves; dropped shoulders.	Sleeveless, strapless and halter-neck styles; tight-fitting, very puffed sleeves.	Remove excess fullness from fitted and set-in sleeves.
THICK WAIST	Hip-length and long jackets; blouson bodices; tunics, overshirts, chemise dresses; dropped, raised waists; narrow waistbands; panelled skirts.	Waistlines, fitted waists on jackets and dresses; wide waistbands; tucked-in blouses; short jackets.	Increase the waist circumference.

Detail	Flattering	Unflattering	Pattern Adjustments
SMALL WAIST	Fitted waistlines; wide waistbands; princess line dresses; fitted, short jackets; cropped tops; midriff inserts.	Unfitted dresses and jackets; long vests, tunics, overshirts, jackets; dropped waists.	Reduce the waist circumference.
FULL HIPS	Loose-fitting overshirts and jackets; below-hip jackets; padded shoulders; straight, A-line, gentle gathers in skirt; trousers with soft gathers at waist, in-seam pockets.	Skirts with stitched-down pleats, darted waists; slant pockets; tight, tapered trousers.	Increase the hip circumference; deepen darts; transform darts to soft gathers.
SMALL HIPS	Gathered, soft pleated skirts; wraparound skirts; trousers with soft pleats.	Tight, straight skirts; jeans; tapered trousers.	Reduce the hip circumference; make waist darts shallower.
FULL THIGHS	Loose trousers hanging straight from hip to floor; skirts with unpressed pleats, bias-cut flares; long tunics, overshirts and jackets.	A-line and straight skirts; tapered trousers; jeans; hip yokes; short jackets.	Increase width of thigh on trousers and skirts.
THIN THIGHS	All skirt styles, culottes, straight-leg or trousers with front pleats.	Jeans and fitted trousers with tapered legs.	Reduce outer side seams, shifting fullness to inner seam.
FULL BUST	Princess seams starting at shoulder; yokes, shoulder seams with gathers, soft pleats; dolman and kimono sleeves; V-necks; darted fronts.	Empire waistlines; wide waistbands; chemise dresses hanging straight from bust without darts; wide double-breasted closings.	Increase bust dart; let out princess seams.
SMALL BUST	Shoulder yokes or seams with gathers or soft pleats; Empire waistlines; double-breasted closings.	Bust darts.	Reduce or eliminate bust darts.

Detail	Flattering	Unflattering	Pattern Adjustments
FULL ABDOMEN	Trousers and skirts with soft pleats, tucks; gathers set to the sides; elasticated waistlines; narrow waist-bands; panelled, bias-cut skirts; chemise dresses; blouson to hips; overshirts; long jackets.	Darted trousers and skirts; wide waistbands; double-breasted closings; fly-front zipper jackets.	Increase centre-front length of trousers and skirts; increase front crotch extension of trousers.
FLAT ABDOMEN	Trousers and skirts with gathers, unpressed pleats; blouson bodices; tunics; dropped waistlines; peplums; chemise dresses.	Tight-fitting trousers and skirts, darted to waistband.	Transform darts to gathers at waist; decrease front crotch length; reduce side seams on fronts of trousers and skirts.
FULL BUTTOCKS	Trousers or skirts with loose fit or unpressed pleats; panelled, flared skirts; long jackets; straight trousers; gathered waistlines; loose tops; chemise dresses.	Close fit above or below waist; tapered pants; dropped waistlines; hip yokes; short jackets.	Increase depth of back waist darts; lengthen back crotch seam on trousers.
FLAT BUTTOCKS	Jumpsuits with waistline; trousers and skirts with pleats, gathers in back or from hip yoke; dirndl, panelled skirts; culottes; harem pants; elasticated back waists; blouson with dropped waistlines.	Tight trousers and skirts; bias-cut skirts.	Remove back waist darts or transform to gathers; shorten back crotch seam.
SWAYBACK BUTTOCKS	Garments with waist seams or with unpressed pleats or gathers; four- or six-panelled skirts; elasticated back waists; boxy jackets to cover back waist.	Hip yokes; short jackets; centre back zips; skirts with stitched or pressed pleats or body-fitting in upper back hip area.	Shorten centre back seam on trousers and skirts.

Measuring Up

The basic body measurements required for selecting a commercial pattern size are bust, waist and hips, although full body measurements will be necessary for any adjustments to these patterns. These will also be needed when making your own patterns. These measurements should be taken accurately, preferably with the help of a friend, and using a non-stretch tape measure. Wear well-fitted undergarments that do not distort your natural body contours. Among the more popular commercial figure type patterns are Misses', Miss Petite, Half-size and Women's.

Pattern Sizes

MISSES' is for the average figure, well-proportioned and about 1.65–1.68 m (5 ft 5 in–5 ft 6 in) tall.

MISS PETITE has a similar shape to Misses', but is shorter in length and about 1.57–1.63 m (5 ft 2 in–5 ft 4 in) tall.

HALF-SIZE is fuller, also with the waist larger in proportion to the bust, the shoulders narrower and the body shorter, and about 1.57–1.6 m (5 ft 2 in–5 ft 3 in) tall.

WOMEN'S is fuller and larger at the bust, waist and hips, but is the same height as Misses', 1.65–1.68 m (5 ft 5 in–5 ft 6 in) tall.

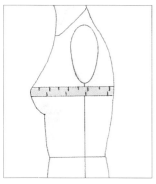

Bust

Around fullest part – about 5 cm (2 in) below armhole.

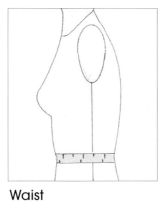

Waist

A fairly snug measurement around waist.

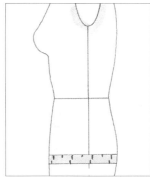

Hip

Around fullest part – about 18 cm (7 in) below waist.

Centre back

Back waist length, from nape of neck to waist.

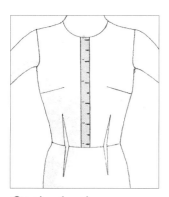

Centre front

From base of neck to waist.

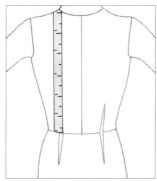

Back shoulder height

From shoulder at neck to waist.

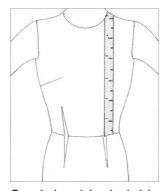

Front shoulder height

From shoulder at neck to waist.

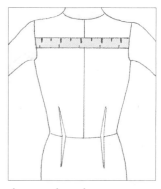

Across back

Armhole to armhole, about 12 cm (5 in) below neck.

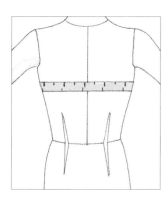

Full back

Side seam to side seam, about 5 cm (2 in) below armhole.

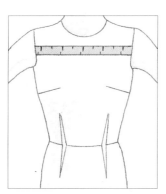

Across front

Armhole to armhole, about 7 cm (3 in) below neck.

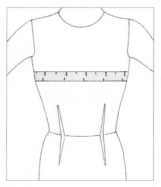

Full front

Across bust from side seam to side seam, 5 cm (2 in) below armhole.

Side seam

From armhole to waist.

37

Personal Touch

Shoulder
From neck to sleeve
crown.

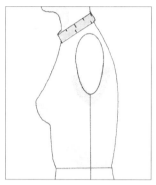

Neck circumference
A fairly loose measurement
around base of neck.

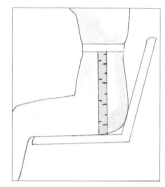

Crotch
Taken in a sitting position
from waist to chair.

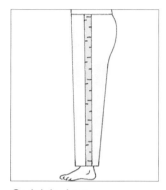

Outside leg
From waist over
hip to ankle.

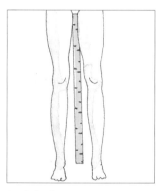

Inside leg
From crotch to inside
of ankle.

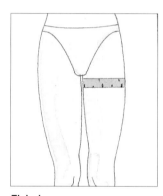

Thigh
Around fullest part of thigh.

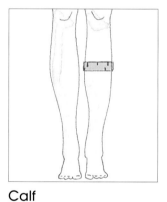

Calf
Around fullest part of calf.

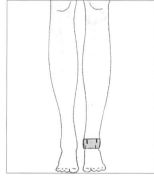

Ankle
Around ankle.

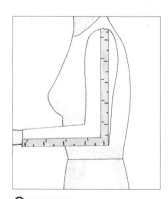

Overarm
From sleeve crown around
bent elbow to wrist.

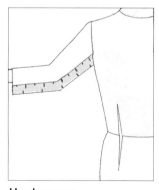

Underarm
From bottom of armhole
to wrist.

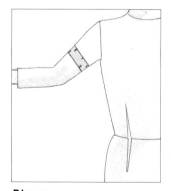

Bicep
Around fullest part of
upper arm.

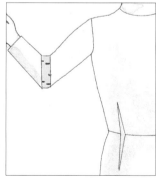

Elbow
Fairly loose measurement
around bent elbow.

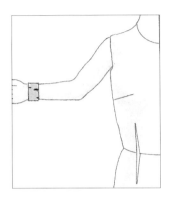

Fitted wrist

A fairly loose measurement around wrist.

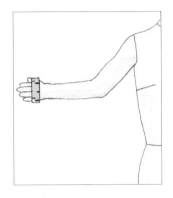

Loose wrist

With fingers together, a fairly snug measurement around broadest part of hand.

International Measurement Chart
These measurements are taken from average bodies and range in size from 32–46 (10–24).
Use this as a guide to your particular size.

Sizes	32 UK 10 US 8		34 UK 12 US 10		36 UK 14 US 12		38 UK 16 US 14		40 UK 18 US 16		42 UK 20 US 18		44 UK 22 US 20		46 UK 24 US 22	
	CM	IN	CM	IN	CM	IN	CM	IN	CM	IN	CM	IN	CM	IN	CM	IN
Bust	82	32	87	34	92	36	97	38	102	40	107	42	112	44	117	46
Waist	61	24	66	26	71	28	76	30	81	32	86	34	91	36	96	38
Hip	87	34	92	36	97	38	102	40	107	42	112	44	117	46	122	48
Neck	36.5	14½	37.5	15	38.5	15½	40	16	41.5	16½	43	17	44.5	17½	46	18
Centre back	41.5	16¼	42	16½	42.5	16¾	43.5	17¼	44	17½	45	17¾	45.5	18	46	18
Front shoulder height	42	16½	43.5	17¼	45	17¾	46	18	47.5	18¾	48.5	19¼	50	19¾	51.5	20¼
Shoulder	12	4¾	12.5	5	13	5¼	13	5¼	13.5	5½	13.5	5½	14	5¾	14.5	5¾
Overarm	58.5	23	59	23¼	59.5	23½	60	23½	60.5	23¾	61	24	61.5	24¼	62	24½
Bicep	28	11	29	11½	30	12	32	12½	34	13½	36	14¼	38	15	40	16
Wrist	15.5	6	16	6¼	16.5	6½	17.5	6¾	18	7	18.5	7¼	19	7½	19.5	7¾
Outside leg	109	43	110	43¼	111	43¾	112	44	113	44½	114	45	115	45¼	116	45¾

Adjusting and customizing patterns

Commercial patterns have various symbols indicating essential fitting points, such as dots, triangles and squares, and double lines for suitable adjustments. To streamline the fitting process, make as many fitting changes as possible prior to cutting.

The following guidelines will assist you when making alterations: for accuracy, press the pattern pieces with a warm, dry iron prior to fitting; pin-fit the pattern and then readjust as required; be sure to match or realign adjoining pattern pieces; maintain the original grainlines throughout; and blend the adjusted stitching and cutting lines to avoid distortion.

A selection of good-quality dressmaking tools will help simplify the task at hand and result in a professional finish.

Pin-fitting Patterns

Pin-fit the pattern to establish how well it fits your figure. In this way the necessary adjustments can be ascertained and you can determine whether another pattern may need to be considered. Double-check by pin-fitting again after adjusting the pattern.

1 Reinforce the neckline and armhole edges of major pattern pieces with lightweight fusible interfacing and clip the curves to the seam line.

4 Fit the pinned pattern on the body, pinning the centre front and back to a close-fitting undergarment and marking the bust point. Determine the necessary adjustments by pinning tucks for excess length and altering seam allowances or repinning darts to increase size.

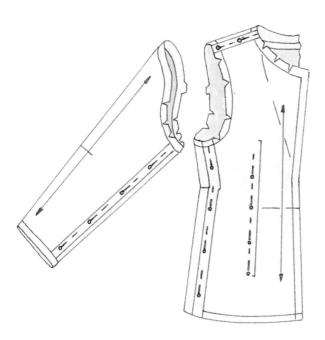

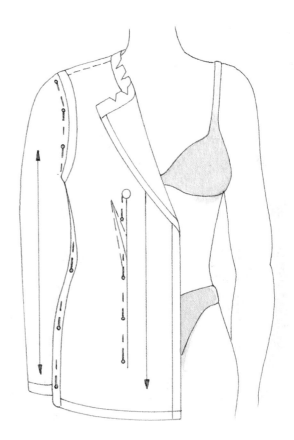

2 Pin darts, pleats or tucks and fold up hems, pinning in place.

3 Lap and pin front and back pattern pieces on sides and shoulders. Repeat on sleeve seams and baste sleeve into armhole.

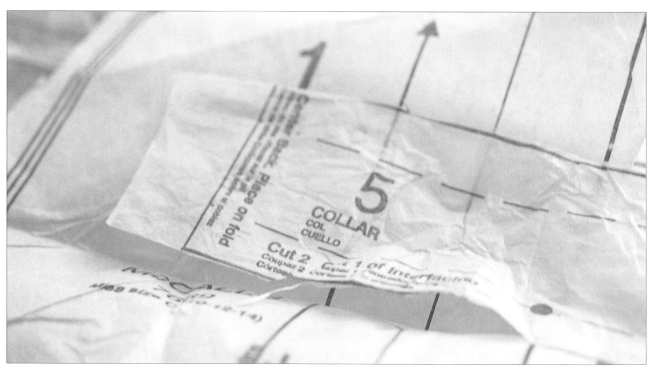

If adjustment lines are omitted from a pattern or are required outside of existing lines, mark a line perpendicular to the centre front or back at the appropriate position. Excess length can be removed from the bottom edge of a garment providing the hem circumference does not alter drastically.

Shortening Patterns

Fold and tape a tuck along the adjustment lines measuring half the required amount. The total amount will be twice the depth. Blend the darts and side seams where necessary.

Lengthening Patterns

Cut the pattern along the adjustment lines and spread the required distance. Place graph or tissue paper underneath to bridge the gap and tape it into position, keeping the grain lines straight. Blend the darts and side seams where necessary.

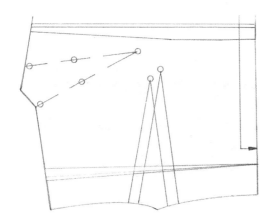

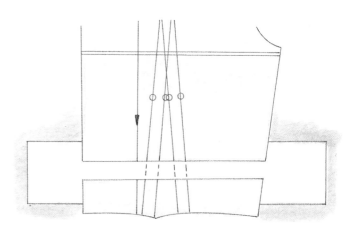

Shoulder Adjustments

It is imperative that the shoulder seams on a pattern fit the width and slope of the body so that the garment can hang correctly from the shoulders and not off-grain. The seams should lie on top of the natural shoulders and appear straight when viewed in profile. Measure your shoulder width from the neck base to the shoulder joint and compare this measurement with your pattern. Pin-fit the pattern to determine the shoulder slope, using shoulder pads if required by the style. Analyze whether any adjustments are necessary.

Sloping Shoulders

This induces wrinkling diagonally from the neckline to the armhole. This can be corrected by inserting shoulder pads or adjusting the shoulder slope of the pattern.

2 Measure the amount pinned away at the end of the shoulder seam and mark this amount down from the shoulder seam on the pattern. Lower the armhole by the same amount.

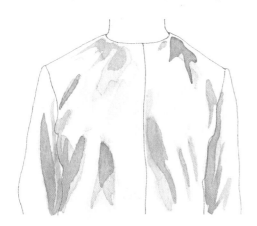

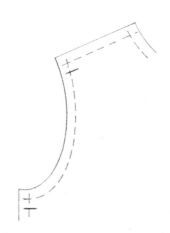

1 Release the pin at the underarm and pin away any excess at the shoulder edge, as illustrated.

3 Blend the stitching and cutting lines, as illustrated. Make the same adjustments on the back and front pattern pieces.

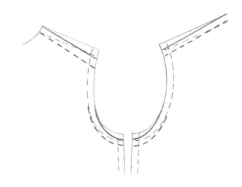

43

Square Shoulders

This will pull up a garment, causing wrinkles across the shoulder area. If a shoulder pad is required, you may avoid adjusting the pattern by inserting a thinner one.

2 Measure the gap at the end of the shoulder and mark half this amount up from the shoulder seam on the front and half on the back. Raise the armholes by the same amount.

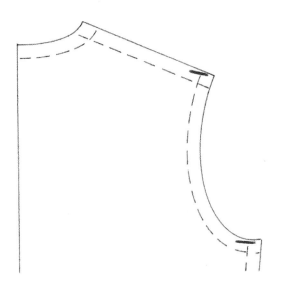

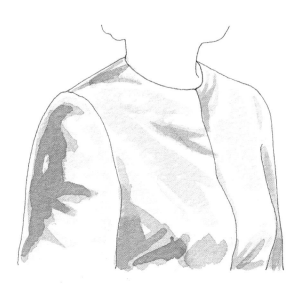

1 Release the pin at the end of the shoulder, keeping the seam together at the neck, as illustrated.

3 Blend the stitching and cutting lines, as illustrated.

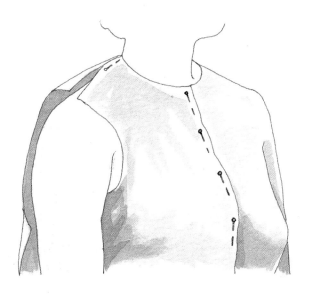

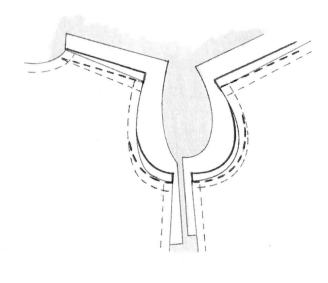

44

Narrow Shoulders

This will cause the armhole seam to extend the natural shoulder seam, making the side of the bodice and the upper sleeve droop and wrinkle. Inserting raglan or rounded shoulder pads can help to reduce the extent of pattern adjustments.

2 Measure the adjustment and mark this amount in from the shoulder seam, as illustrated.

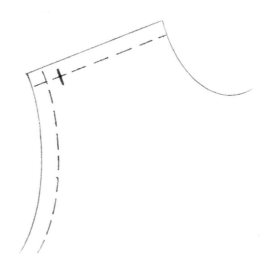

3 Blend the stitching and cutting lines of the armhole. Make matching adjustments to the back and front patterns.

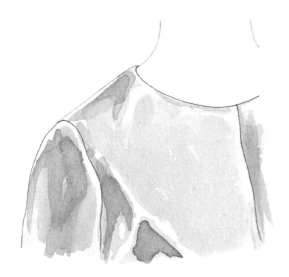

1 Pin the excess at the shoulder/armhole seam so that the shoulder seam ends at the shoulder joint.

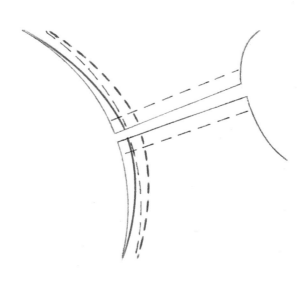

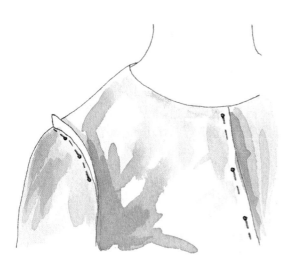

Broad Shoulders

This will pull the top of the sleeves tight across the shoulder, causing the sleeve to fall off-grain and wrinkling the fabric. The shoulder seam must be extended.

2 Draw a line through the shoulder end perpendicular to the centre back, as illustrated. Mark the shoulder length to cross this line. The lengthened shoulder seam will be slightly raised.

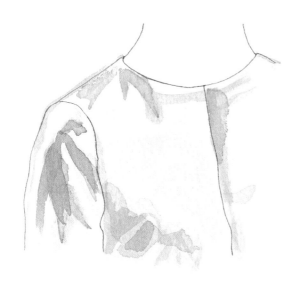

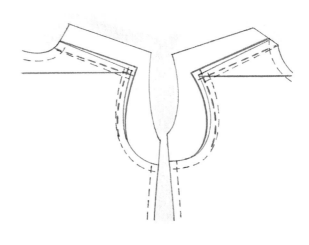

1 Measure the length of the shoulder from the neck to the shoulder joint, as illustrated on page 38.

3 Blend the stitching and cutting lines of the armhole. Adjust the back and front alike.

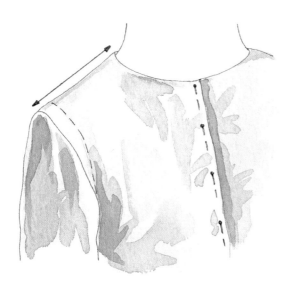

Forward Thrust Shoulders

This will cause set-in sleeves to wrinkle and feel uncomfortable. This will result in wrinkling at the neckline and at the back of the armholes.

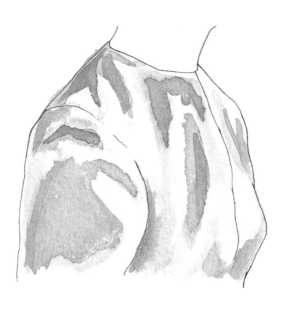

1 Pin-fit the pattern and view the shoulder seam in profile to ascertain how much the shoulder seam is pulling towards the back.

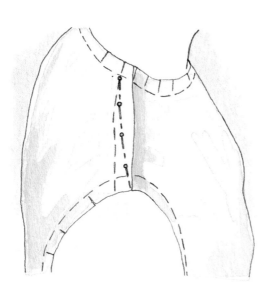

2 Reposition the shoulder seam so that it falls straight. Drop the shoulder end on the front and raise it on the back according to the refit, as illustrated.

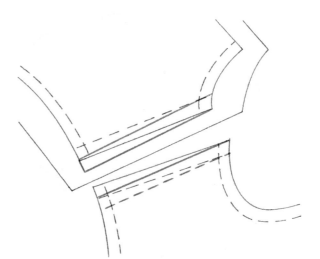

3 Shift the shoulder notch on the sleeve to coincide with the shoulder adjustment.

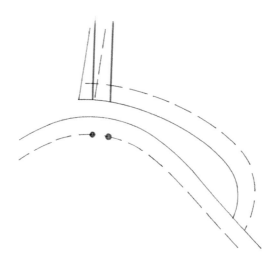

Neckline Adjustments

The fit of the neckline, as with the shoulder seam, is of prime importance. It frames the face and also influences the fall of the garment. To fit correctly, it should lie smoothly against the body without wrinkling or gaping. First fit the neckline, then adjust the facings and collars accordingly. Adjustments are usually small, no greater than 10–12 mm (⅜–½ in). Exceeding these amounts will only complicate adjusting adjacent pattern pieces.

After adjusting the shoulder seam, pin-fit the pattern to analyze the neckline. The front of the neckline should rest on the collarbone and may be raised or lowered to improve the fit.

The neckline at the shoulder seam should rest on the neck base in line with the ear lobe. It can be made wider or narrower at the shoulder for a better fit. The adjustments discussed below apply to the basic, fitted, round neckline, with or without a collar.

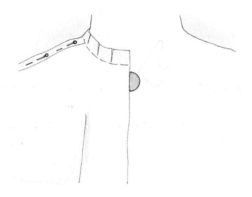

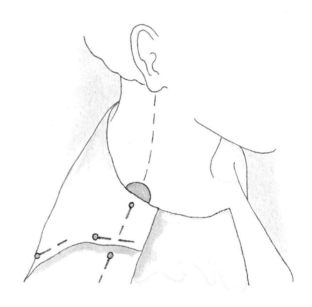

The centre back of the neckline should rest on the prominent bone at the base of the neck and may also be raised or lowered as required.

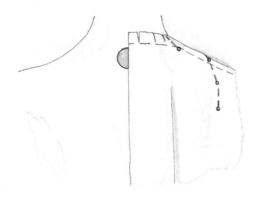

To find your neck base, tilt your head to the side and note where your skin creases.

48

A Neckline Too High

This will cause wrinkling, strain the fabric and pull it off-grain. The neckline will feel tight and rest above the neck base. This problem occurs more commonly at the front of the garment.

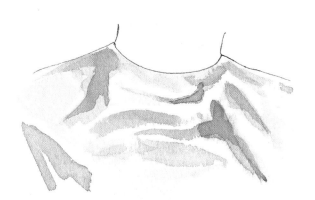

Lower the neckline at the centre front as required, but by no more than 1 cm (⅜ in) if a collar is to be attached. Blend this new line into the original neckline, squaring it slightly at the centre front to maintain a smooth curve. Follow this same method when the back needs to be raised.

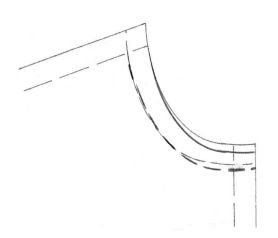

A Neckline Too Low

This is a problem more commonly found at the back, causing the neckline to gape.

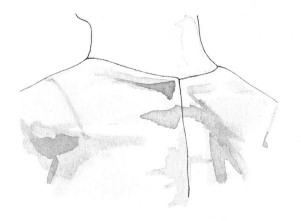

Raise the neckline at the centre back as required, but by no more than 1 cm (⅜ in). Square this new line across to intersect the original neckline and blend the curve, as illustrated. The same method can be used to adjust the back and front.

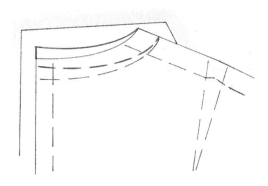

49

A Neckline Too Wide

This will make the garment seem too large and the neckline seam will fall short at the shoulders.

A Neckline Too Narrow

This will appear to be a problem at the shoulder as it causes similar diagonal wrinkles from the neck to the armhole. It will also pull the neckline upwards.

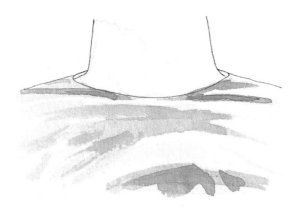

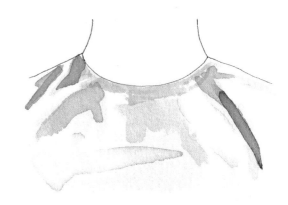

Square a line from the centre front through the shoulder/ neckline intersection. Mark the new crossing point on this line closer to the centre front to reduce the neckline width. Adjust the angle of the shoulder seam and blend the new neckline. Add no more than 1 cm (⅜ in) to small sizes and 12 mm (½ in) to large sizes.

Square a line from the centre front through the shoulder/ neckline intersection. Mark the new crossing point on this line but further away from the centre front to increase the neckline width. Adjust the angle of the shoulder seam and blend the new neckline. A maximum of 1 cm (⅜ in) can be removed from small sizes and 12 mm (½ in) from large sizes.

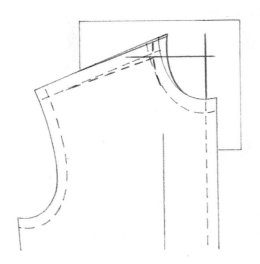

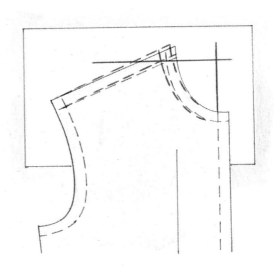

Collars and Facings

These need to be adjusted to coincide with any neckline alterations. Facings can be remade using the new neckline and the depth of the original facing pattern, as illustrated.

Collars, flat, convertible and two-piece, should be divided into four equal sections and either spread or overlapped evenly to comply with the neckline alterations, as illustrated.

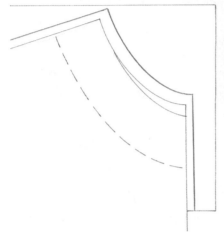

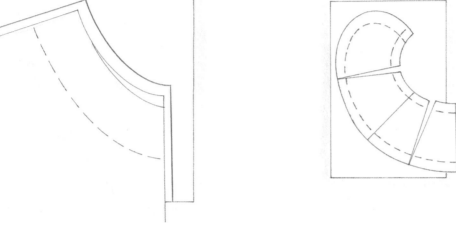

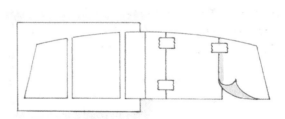

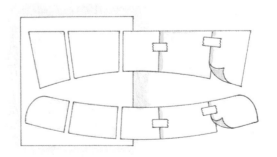

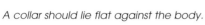

A collar should lie flat against the body.

Bust Adjustments

The bodice of a garment should fit smoothly across the bust without pulling the waistline up or the side seams forward. At times the bust darts may require adjustments to achieve a perfect fit. Pin-fitting the pattern is suitable for small to average busts where repositioning the darts may be all that is required, but making a calico mock-up of the bodice may be necessary to test the adjustments on larger busts.

A small amount of ease should be added to your bust measurement to ensure a comfortable fit at the bust-line. Use the chart below as a guide to adding the required amount to your bust measurement before comparing it to the pattern. Bear in mind that thick fabrics require more ease than lightweight ones; knits less than wovens; and very stretchy knits such as Lycra, no ease at all. Fuller figures may require more ease for added comfort.

Keep the tape measure level when measuring the bust and add the required ease. Measure the side-front length from the centre of the shoulder over the bust point and down to the waist. Using two fingers to determine the underarm position, measure the side length from the underarm to the waist. Pin-fit the pattern to ascertain the bust point. Compare the body measurements to the pattern measurements to determine the necessary adjustments.

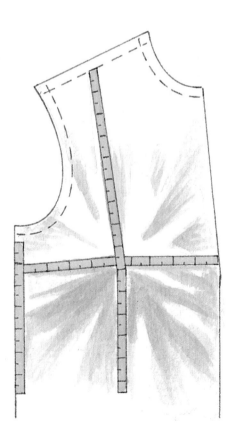

Garment	Minimum Bust Ease
Shirt, dress, jumpsuit	6.5–7.5 cm (2½–3 in)
Unlined jacket	7.5–10 cm (3–4 in)
Lined jacket	9–11.5 cm (3½–4½ in)
Coat	10–12.5 cm (4–5 in)

52

A High or Low Bust

This can distort the fit, pulling the garment across the bust and causing wrinkles below the bust on a high bust, and above the bust on a low bust.

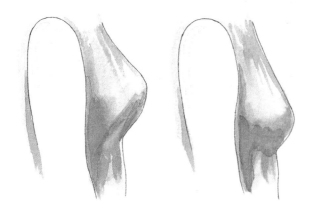

1 Mark the new bust point. Draw horizontal lines, perpendicular to the grain line, 12 mm (½ in) above and below the underarm bust dart. Draw a vertical line through the dart point, as illustrated, and cut out the dart along these marked lines.

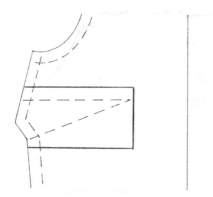

2a For a high bust, raise the dart by sliding the cut-out panel along the vertical line so that the dart points to the new bust point. Place tissue paper or interfacing under the pattern, and tape it into position. Redraw the side seam, blend the edges and trim off any excess.

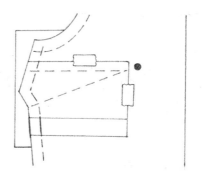

2b For a low bust, lower the dart by sliding the cut-out panel along the vertical line so that the dart points to the new bust point. Place interfacing under the pattern and tape it in position. Redraw the side seam, blend the edges and trim off any excess.

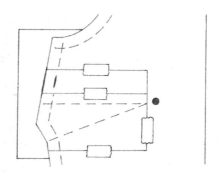

3 To alter the direction of a diagonal dart, redraw from the side seam ends of the dart to the new bust point.

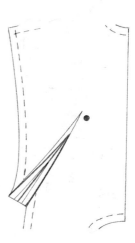

A Full Bust

This will push the bodice up in front and the side seams forward. To combat this, the dart can be enlarged and the front length increased or, if no darts are supplied, a dart can be created. Alternatively, the across-bust measurement and the centre-front length can be increased, maintaining the same side seam length and tapering it to the original waist measurement.

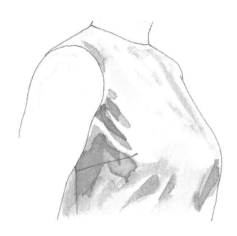

1 To enlarge the dart, draw a line from the side seam through the centre of the dart to the bust point and then perpendicular to the centre front, as illustrated. Draw a second line from the armhole notch to the bust point and then to the waist, keeping this section parallel to the grain line.

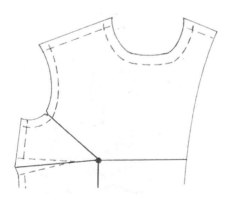

2 Place paper or interfacing under the pattern and cut from the waist to the bust point and to, but not through, the armhole notch. Cut from the centre front to the bust point and then along the line from the side seam to, but not through, the bust point, as illustrated.

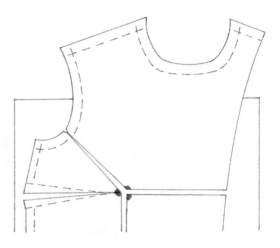

3 Spread the pattern by half the required amount: C-cup 12 mm (½ in); D-cup 2 cm (¾ in); larger than D-cup 3.2 cm (1¼ in). Keep the side panel parallel to the grain line and slide the centre panel down so that the waist seam lines correspond, as illustrated.

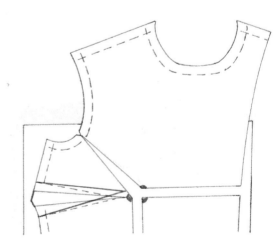

54

4 Draw the new dart fold line from the side seam to the bust point and mark the stitch lines to meet about 5–6.5 cm (2–2½ in) from the bust point. Fold the dart and blend the side and waist seams.

5 To create a dart, draw a line at the desired angle from the side seam to the bust point and through to the centre front as in step 1. Continue the same adjustments from step 2 to step 4, marking the new dart as illustrated.

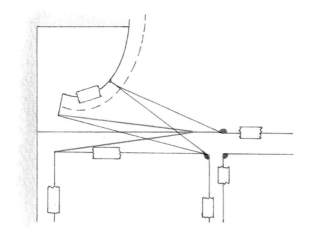
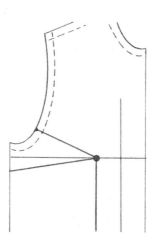

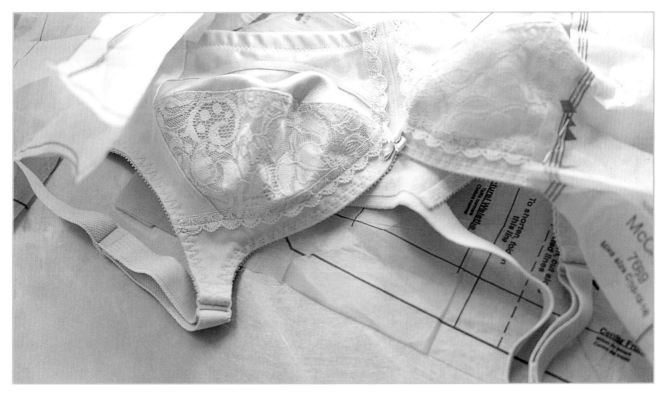

A full bust requires a good-fitting bra. This will make all the difference to the fit of a garment.

A Gaping Armhole

This can be eliminated by supressing the shoulder seam at the armhole, by inserting a shoulder pad or by adding a dart to the armhole.

1 Pin-fit the excess amount from the centre of the armhole to the bust.

2 Mark the stitch lines and blend the cutting line, as illustrated. Open the dart.

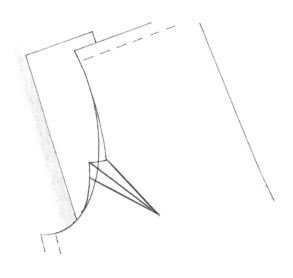

3 If a sleeve is required, cut across the sleeve cap to reduce the ease by the same amount as the dart depth. For sleeves with small amounts of ease, this adjustment can be eliminated.

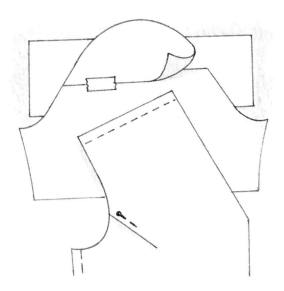

A Small Bust

This requires only shallow darts, if any at all. If the darts are too deep and shapely for the small contours of the bust, the garment can easily look baggy. Reduce the bust dart as required, marking the stitching lines inside the original lines. Adjust the side seam to compensate for this alteration.

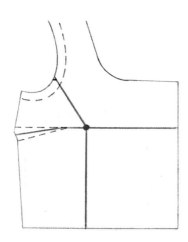

1 Eliminate the bust dart by drawing a line through the centre of the dart to the bust point and then perpendicular to the centre front. Draw another line from the armhole notch through the bust point and down to the waist, keeping this line parallel to the grain line.

2 Place interfacing under the pattern and cut the line from the waist to the bust point and then to, but not through, the armhole notch. Cut from the centre front to the bust point and then from the side seam to, but not through, the bust point, as illustrated.

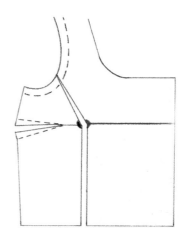

3 Slide the side-front pattern inwards, closing most of the dart: A-cup or smaller, 12 mm (½ in). Slide the centre-front panel upwards until the waist seam lines correspond. Tape into position. Compare the side seam lengths on the front and back and adjust the front accordingly.

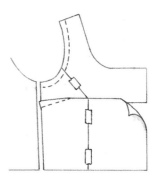

Princess Seams

These are simple to adjust and make bust fitting easy. Whether the seams come from the shoulder or the armhole, the adjustments are the same. Pin-fit the pattern to see where the seam shapes the bustline, and to determine the bust point.

A High or Low Bust

This can easily be altered. Draw a line through the bust point perpendicular to the grain line on both fronts. Cut through these lines and overlap for a high bust or spread for a low bust, as required. Compensate for the change in length by cutting through the pattern's adjustment lines and spreading for a high bust or overlapping for a low bust, as illustrated.

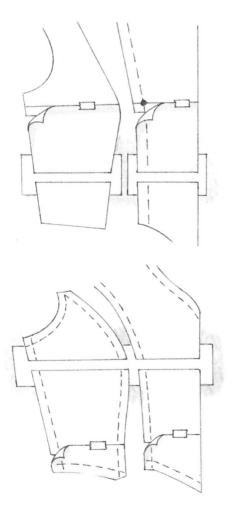

A Full Bust

This can be adjusted by adding 6 mm (¼ in) for each bra-cup size larger than B, to the fullest part of the bust-line curve on the side front panel. Blend the stitch lines and cutting lines to 10 cm (4 in) above and below the bust point. Lengthen the centre-front panel by cutting a line through at the bust point perpendicular to the centre front and spreading the pattern 6 mm (¼ in) for each bra-cup size, corresponding to the side panel.

A Small Bust

This can be adjusted by following the same instructions as for a full bust, but in this instance removing 6 mm (¼ in) from the bustline curve and overlapping the centre-front panel by 6 mm (¼ in), as illustrated.

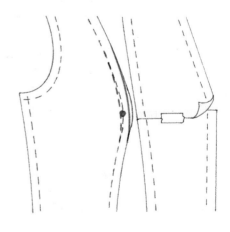

Back Adjustments

A garment needs to fit well across the back to ensure wearing comfort. Whether the arms are straight at the sides or folded in front, the garment should fit smoothly across the back without straining the armhole seams or fabric. Poor posture will also result in fitting problems across the back. Shoulder darts must be added for a rounded back and, in extreme cases, neckline darts may be required. The centre-back length will need to be extended to accommodate these contours.

Ease across the back is essential for added comfort. Use the chart below as a guide to adding the necessary ease to your across-back measurement before comparing it to the pattern. Sleeveless garments require less ease than sleeved styles; thick fabrics will require more ease than thin, lightweight ones; knits require less than wovens; and stretchy knits, such as Lycra, require no ease at all. Fuller figures may require more ease for added comfort.

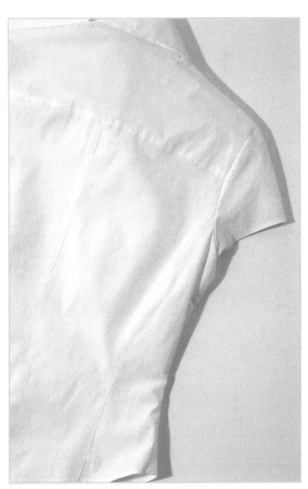

Garment	Minimum Back Ease
Shirt, dress, sleeveless jumpsuit	12 mm–2.5 cm (½–1 in)
Jumpsuit with sleeves	2.5 cm (1 in)
Jacket	2.5–3.8 cm (1–1½ in)
Coat	2.5–5 cm (1–2 in)

Measure the back width from arm crease to arm crease, about 10–15 cm (4–6 in) below the bone at the base of the neck, and add the required ease. Measure the back waist length from the neck bone to the waist. Compare both these measurements with the pattern. When you have made the required adjustments, pin-fit the pattern to ascertain the need for any dart positioning for a rounded back or for protruding shoulder blades.

The back of a garment should fit smoothly and comfortably without straining any seams.

A Narrow Back

This will generally make the garment seem too big and will cause the front to fall off-grain.

Reduce the across-back measurement by removing 6 mm–2.5 cm (¼–1 in) from each armhole on smaller sizes, and 1–3.8 cm (⅜–1½ in) on larger sizes, as required. Remove an equal amount from the side seams at the underarm, as illustrated. Blend the stitching and cutting lines.

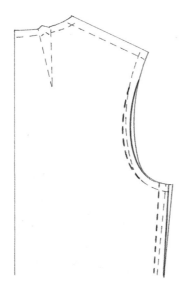

A Broad Back

This will induce wrinkling across the sleeve cap, which in turn will pull the garment backwards and create an uncomfortable fit.

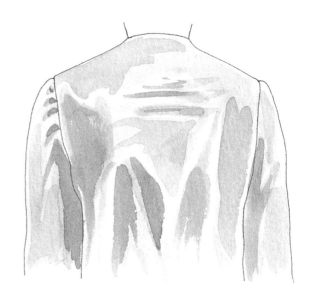

Increase the across-back measurement by adding 6 mm–2.5 cm (¼–1 in) to each armhole on smaller sizes, and 1–3.8 cm (⅜–1½ in) on larger sizes, as required. Add an equal amount to the side seams at the under-arm, as illustrated. Blend the stitching and cutting lines.

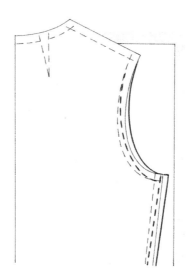

A Rounded Back

This will create horizontal wrinkles below the back neckline, pulling the garment up at the back waistline and resulting in an uneven hem. The back needs to be lengthened and shoulder darts added.

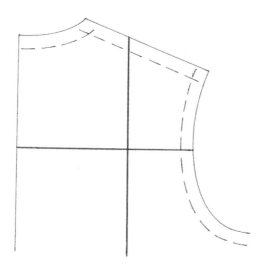

1 Draw a perpendicular line about 10 cm (4 in) below the neck from the centre back to the armhole. Draw another line parallel to the grain line from the centre of the shoulder or shoulder dart (if any), to the perpendicular line.

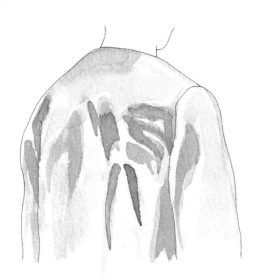

2 Cut from the centre back to, but not through, the armhole. Cut from the shoulder to, but not through the adjustment line. Place paper under the pattern and slide the top section upwards, as required, keeping the centre back parallel to the grain line. The dart will form as the shoulder section tilts outwards. Tape into position.

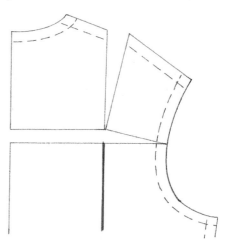

3 Blend the centre-back line and fold the dart to blend the stitching and cutting lines at the shoulders. Generally, the dart is about 7.5 cm (3 in) long, but pin-fit to shorten or lengthen as required.

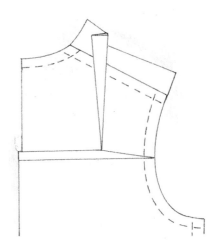

A Very High Rounded Back

Also known as a dowager's hump, this is often found on an elderly person. A protrusion is formed below the neck base and this causes the neckline to stand away at the back, pulling on the front. A dart needs to be added to the back neck to create a proper fit.

1 Draw a perpendicular line about 10 cm (4 in) below the neck from the centre back to the armhole. Draw another line parallel to the grain line from the centre of the neck to the perpendicular line. Add up to 3.8 cm (1½ in) seam allowance to the centre back if the pattern is cut on the fold.

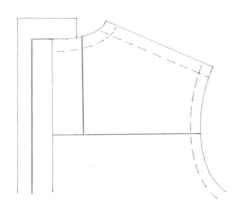

2 Cut from the centre back to, but not through, the armhole. Cut from the neckline to, but not through, the adjustment line. Place paper under the pattern and slide the top section upwards, as required, keeping the centre back parallel to the grain line. The dart will form as the shoulder section tilts outwards. Tape into position.

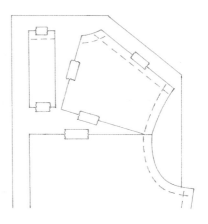

3 Blend the centre-back line and fold the neck dart to blend the stitching and cutting lines at the neck. Pin-fit the pattern to ascertain the dart length and to check whether the centre back needs further adjustment.

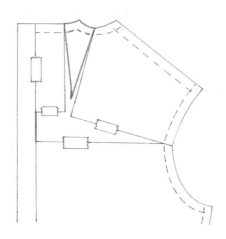

Sleeve Adjustments

A well-fitted sleeve rests on the wristbone when the arm is slightly bent, and should fit around the upper arm without any strain. Gathered sleeves require extra length for blousing; coat sleeves should cover the sleeves of the garment worn underneath; and jacket sleeves should be slightly shorter to expose the shirt or dress cuff. Bear in mind that shoulder pads shorten the sleeve length and adjustments may be required. The sleeve should drape slightly forwards when the arm is relaxed.

Ease is again essential for sleeves to fit comfortably. Use the chart below as a guide to adding the necessary ease to the upper-arm measurement before comparing it to the pattern. Set-in sleeves may fit closely, requiring adjustment only for fabric type; thick fabric requires more ease than a thin, flimsy one; knits less than wovens; and very stretchy knits, such as Lycra, none at all. Large arms may require more ease than usual, thus selecting a style with fuller-cut sleeves would be more suitable.

Garment	Minimum Upper Arm Ease
Shirt, blouse	2.5–3.8 cm (1–1½ in)
Dress, jumpsuit	3.8–5 cm (1½–2 in)
Unlined jacket	7.5–10 cm (3–4 in)
Lined jacket	7.5–11.5 cm (3–4½ in)
Coat	10–14 cm (4–5½ in)

Measure the circumference of the upper arm and add the required amount of ease. With your arm slightly bent, measure the arm length from the shoulder to the wristbone, taking note of the elbow position. Compare these measurements to the pattern and adjust accordingly.

Sleeves may vary in length and width, but be sure to allow enough ease to avoid any strain on the armhole.

Full Arms

This will cause wrinkling if insufficient ease is included. The sleeve will be uncomfortable to wear and could easily rip at the armhole seam. This is commonly found on traditional set-in sleeves.

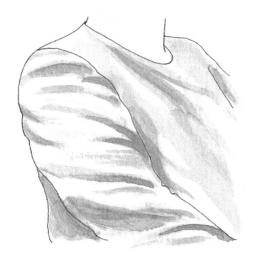

1 For a small adjustment, add 1 cm (⅜ in) at the underarm to each side seam, and blend to the original seams.

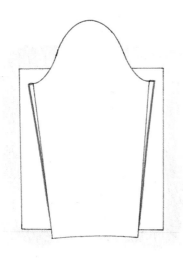

2 For a substantial adjustment, draw a line 2.5 cm (1 in) above the notches and 5 cm (2 in) below the under-arm, both perpendicular to the grain line and parallel to each other. Divide the top line into three equal parts and draw two lines parallel to the grain line.

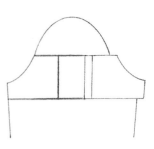

3 Cut along these lines, as illustrated, and place paper under the pattern. Spread the sleeve cap sections equally, adding 3.8 cm (1½ in) to each side. Tape into position.

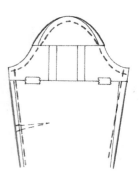

4 Blend the stitching and cutting lines and measure the sleeve cap and armhole between the notches. The sleeve cap ease should not be more than 2.5 cm (1 in) for firm fabrics, or 3.8–5 cm (1½–2 in) for soft and loose weaves. Adjust shoulder and underarm seams equally to compensate for the new sleeve cap. Insert shoulder pads for a better fit.

Thin Arms

This seldom presents problems to the fit of a sleeve, but excess ease may cause the sleeve to droop and form folds in the upper arm area.

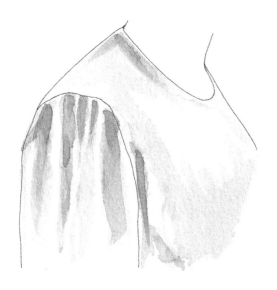

This can be eliminated by trimming the side seams at the underarm or by inserting a shoulder pad to support the sleeve cap. Avoid over-adjusting as this will only call attention to the thin upper arm.

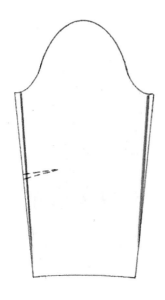

Sleeve Lengths

Sleeves can be adjusted by spreading or overlapping on the printed adjustment lines. A shirt sleeve requires one adjustment;

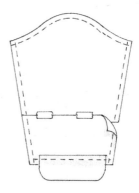

a fitted sleeve with an elbow dart will need equal adjustment above and below the dart;

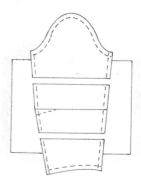

a two-piece jacket sleeve will need equal adjustment above and below the elbow curve.

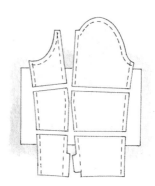

Waist, Abdomen and Hip Adjustments

All waistlines should fit snugly, but for wearing comfort 12 mm–2 cm (½–¾ in) ease must be added to the waist measurement. Larger sizes require about 2.5 cm (1 in) ease. A sure indication of sufficient ease would be whether the side seams hang straight without being pulled to the back or front. A full abdomen requires a larger front waist measurement and a swayback needs a smaller back waist measurement, as well as shortening the centre-back length. All garments should hang smoothly around the hipline. Ease of 5–6.5 cm (2–2½ in) should be added to hip measurements for the garment to fit comfortably, bearing in mind that thicker fabrics will require more ease than finer or stretch fabrics.

Measure the waist and add the required ease. Measure the hips 20 cm (8 in) down from the waist and add the required ease. Pin any darts or tucks in the pattern before comparing the measurements, and adjust accordingly.

Fitted waists should fit snugly with sufficient ease.

Tracksuit pants have an elasticized waist for added comfort.

A Small Waist

This will cause the waistline seam on a dress to bag, and the waistband on trousers or a skirt will stand away from the waist and tend to slide down.

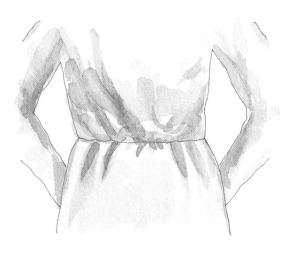

Remove a quarter of the excess amount from each side seam at the waist, tapering to the hip. Do not make any darts deeper to reduce the waistline unless the hips are broad and curvy or the buttocks full and rounded. Adjust corresponding patterns accordingly.

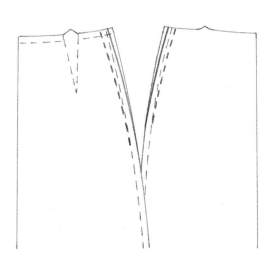

A Thick Waist

This will push the garment upwards, causing horizontal wrinkles at the waist.

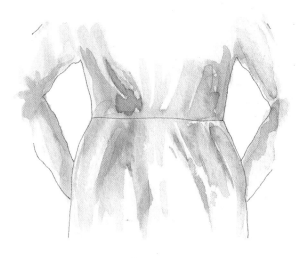

Add a quarter of the required amount to the waist on each side seam, tapering to the hip. To increase the waist on darted garments, the darts may be reduced by 6 mm (¼ in). Adjust any corresponding patterns accordingly.

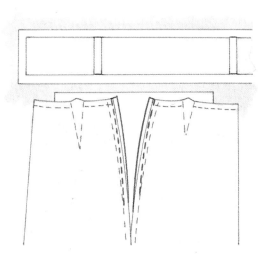

67

A Full Abdomen

This causes diagonal wrinkles across the front from the abdomen to the sides, pulling the side seams forward. A skirt will ride up at the hemline and waistline and trousers will pull up in the crotch. (See trouser adjustments on page 72.)

1 The centre front can be lengthened by 1 cm (⅜ in) at the waist and widened by 12 mm (½ in) at each side seam. Remove the same amount from the back side seams to maintain the waist circumference.

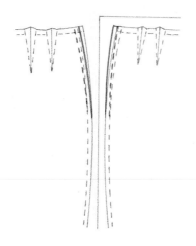

2 For larger adjustments, draw a line from the waist at the side seam, through the dart points, and then perpendicular to the centre front, as illustrated.

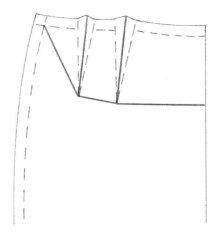

3 Cut this line from the centre front to, but not through, the waist/side-seam intersection. Cut the centre of the dart to, but not through, the dart point. Slide the centre section up as required, keeping the centre front parallel to the grain line and bridging the gap with paper. The darts and the diagonal slash will spread automatically. Tape into position, blending the stitching and cutting lines. Convert the darts to unpressed pleats.

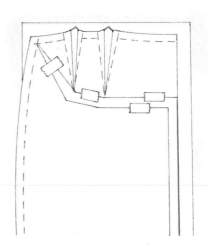

A Flat Abdomen

This will cause vertical wrinkles and, invariably, the darts will be badly positioned and too deep.

Redraw shallower darts, compensating at each side seam for this amount. The darts can also be moved closer to the side seam for prominent hipbones.

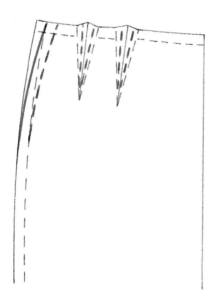

Swayback Buttocks

This will cause wrinkles that are deeper at the back than at the side seams. The lower back looks hollowed, showing that the centre back of the garment is too long above the hips – darts seem to emphasize this.

Lower the back waist by 12 mm–2 cm (½–¾ in) at the centre, tapering to the sides. This applies to skirts and trousers alike. Any back darts should be shortened on trousers or converted into soft gathers on skirts.

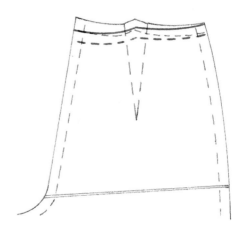

Full Hips

This will create horizontal wrinkles on a fitted skirt and will push it upwards.

Extend the hipline at the side seams on the back and front, adding up to 1 cm (⅜ in) on each seam. Blend the stitching and cutting lines from the hip to the waist, and from the hip straight down to the hem, as illustrated.

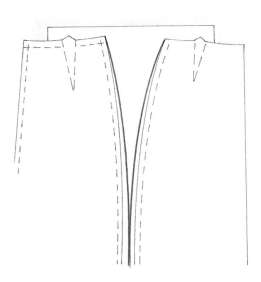

Small Hips

This will make a skirt look baggy, causing excess fabric to drape in folds.

Reduce the hipline by removing a quarter of the required amount from each side seam at the hip. Blend the stitching and cutting lines to nothing at the waist and hem. The waist darts may have to be reduced, depending on the individual.

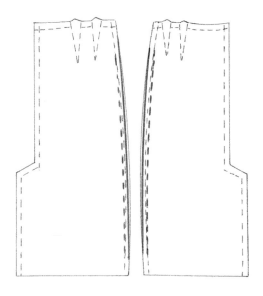

Trouser Adjustments

Trousers should hang straight from the hips to the hem without wrinkling, pulling or sagging. The seams should be perpendicular to the floor, not tilted to the front or back. Above all, the trousers should be comfortable to wear. The same waist and hip adjustments apply to both skirts and trousers. The other areas of importance to a good-fitting pair of trousers are the crotch, buttocks and thighs. Initially, a trial garment will simplify the fitting of trousers and assist with ascertaining the necessary adjustments.

Comfortable trousers require wearing ease. Tight-fitting jeans will require less ease than jumpsuits or trousers with soft pleats; larger sizes will require more ease. Use the chart below as a guide to adding ease to your measurements.

Area	Minimum Ease
Crotch depth	12 mm (½ in) for small sizes
	2 cm (¾ in) for medium sizes
	2.5 cm (1 in) for large sizes
Crotch length	2.5–5 cm (1–2 in)
Waist	2–2.5 cm (¾–1 in)
Hips	5–6.5 cm (2–2½ in)
Thighs	5 cm (2 in)

Add the necessary ease before comparing it to the pattern. Adjust the length accordingly, by either overlapping or spreading at the adjustment line. Measure the crotch length by taking the through-body measurement from the front waist to the back waist. Add the required ease before comparing it to the pattern. Likewise, add the ease to the thigh measurement before comparison.

Sit on a hard, flat surface, keeping your feet flat on the floor, and measure the side length from the waist to the surface to determine the crotch depth.

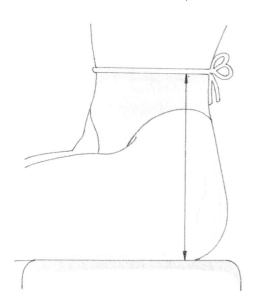

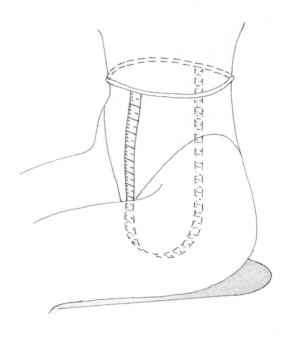

71

A Full Abdomen

This will create horizontal wrinkles across the lower abdomen and thighs, and will pull the back seam forward because of the short front crotch. For a small alteration, follow the same instructions for skirts on page 68.

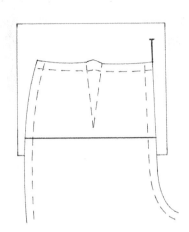

1 For substantial alterations, place paper under the pattern and extend the front-crotch seam by 5 cm (2 in) above the waist. Draw an adjustment line halfway down the crotch, perpendicular to the grain line.

2 Cut along this line from the centre front to, but not through, the side seam. Raise the centre front as required and tape into position.

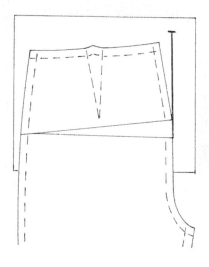

3 Extend the waistline to the raised centre-front line, maintaining the original curve, and blend the side seam.

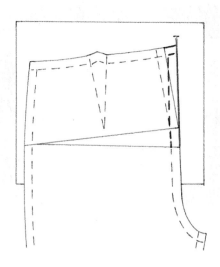

Full Buttocks

This will create diagonal wrinkles, pulling the inside seams upwards and the waistband down. The back crotch length needs to be extended.

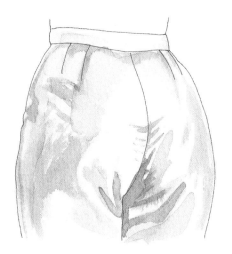

1 The back crotch curve can be extended by 12 mm (½ in) and the inside seam blended into the original seam, as illustrated.

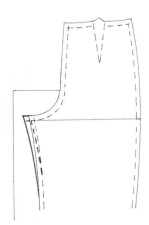

2 For a substantial adjustment, draw horizontal lines 10 cm (4 in) above and below the crotch line, perpendicular to the grain line. Connect these two lines with a vertical line, parallel to the grain line.

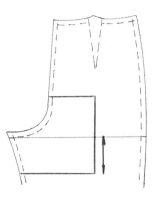

3 Cut along these lines and slide out the cut-out, keeping the crotch line straight. Add on 2.5–3.8 cm (1–1½ in) depending on the size.

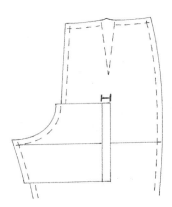

4 Bridge the gap with paper and blend the crotch seam up to the waist, and the inside seam to the knee. Make this adjustment to the back only.

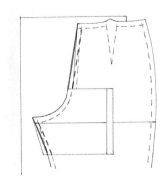

73

Flat Buttocks

This will cause the trousers to sag below the crotch at the back of the legs. The crotch seam is too long for the flat contours of the buttocks, creating excess fabric at the back.

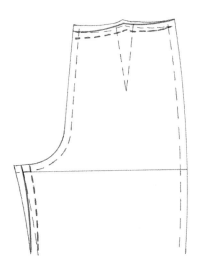

1 To shorten the crotch seam slightly, remove half the amount from the waistline and half from the crotch extension, as illustrated. Blend the stitching and cutting lines.

2 Draw adjustment lines as for full buttocks, step 2. Slide in the cut-out to shorten the crotch seam. Stop adjusting when the inside seam runs straight.

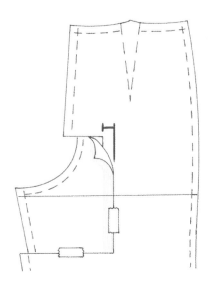

3 Shorten the balance of the crotch at the waistline seam. Remove a total of 3.8–6.5 cm (1½–2½ in), depending on size. Bridge the gap with paper, tape into position and blend the stitching and cutting lines. Alter only the back.

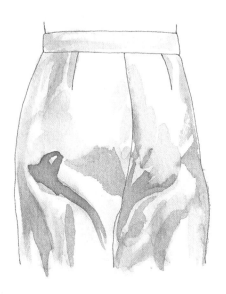

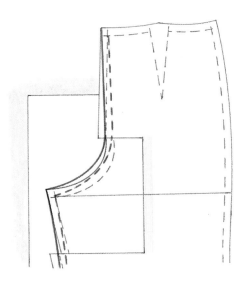

Thin Thighs

This will cause trousers to bag at the thighs, creating vertical wrinkles.

Trim a quarter of the required amount from each seam: on the inside seam, from the crotch down; and on the side seam, from the crotch line down, blending up to the hip, as illustrated.

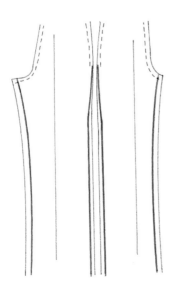

Full Thighs

This creates wrinkles across the thigh, upper inside seam and side seam. The trousers will cup under the buttocks and pull the front creases towards the outer seam.

Place paper under the pattern and extend side and inside seams by a quarter of the required amount. Make these adjustments to the backs and fronts. Blend the side seams, curving gently up to the hips and straight down to the hem. Blend inside seams from the crotch to the hem. Ensure that back and front seams correspond.

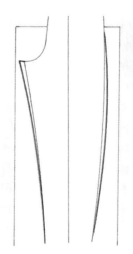

Full Inner Thighs

This will create diagonal wrinkles running up from the inside seams. The fabric will pull inwards, causing the trousers to hang off-grain. Full buttocks usually accompany this problem (see page 73).

Add sufficient ease to ensure that trousers lie smoothly across the thighs without any wrinkling.

1 Draw an adjustment line at the knee, perpendicular to the grain line. Cut this line and slide the lower panel towards the inside seam, adding the required amount. Stop adding to the width when the inside seam is perpendicular to the crotch point. Blend the side and inside seams, bridging the gap with paper, and tape into place.

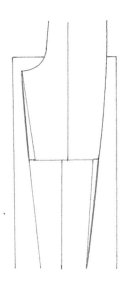

2 Fold the patterns vertically in half to mark the new grain line, matching the side and inside seams. Adjust both the back and front.

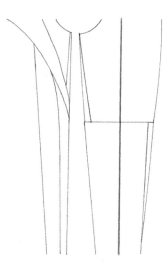

Full Outer Thighs

This will cause diagonal wrinkles at the front, pulling up the fabric at the sides because the trousers are not wide enough for the full outer thigh contours.

1 Draw an adjustment line 2.5 cm (1 in) above the crotch line and another 10–15 cm (4–6 in) below the crotch line, both lines perpendicular to the grain line. Connect these lines vertically 2.5 cm (1 in) off the centre of the panel and parallel to the grain line.

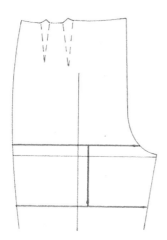

2 Cut along these lines and slide out the cut-out to half the required amount. Blend the seam line above to the hipline and below to the hem. Match corresponding adjustments to the back and front.

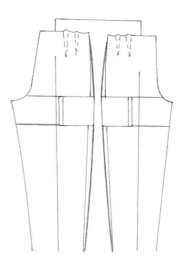

Trouser Lengths

The length can be adjusted by drawing a line perpendicular to the grain line below the knee, and spreading or overlapping as required.

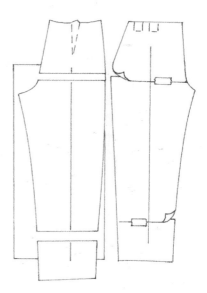

77

chapter four

Dressing your figure

Fundamental knowledge of sewing and the discipline to assemble a garment in the correct order will result in a professional-looking garment. Care must be taken to execute the various techniques with the utmost accuracy. The secret lies in fitting and pressing. Devote time to these steps and you will benefit greatly. After all, classic garments should not look home-made. Finishes such as darts, tucks, collars and cuffs need to be completed before stitching them into their respective positions. Once this is completed and any zips have been attached, the garment is ready for its final assembly. Linings can be inserted and, ultimately, buttons added.

T-SHIRT

T-shirts are generally made in cotton knit or various similar knits. They may be single jersey or double knit, honeycomb or plain – almost any knit will do providing the fabric is of a good quality. Bear in mind that the heavier the knit, the more body it will have and ultimately, the smarter it will look. However, lightweight mercerized cotton knit also has a rich appearance. The T-shirt neckline can be round, boat-necked or V-necked, and is usually trimmed with ribbing. It can also be bound in self fabric or another contrast cloth depending on the effect required. Mitre the V-neck carefully to prevent it from pulling to one side.

1 Select a suitable T-shirt pattern and pin-fit before cutting to check for any possible adjustments (see pages 41–65).

2 Select the relevant fabric, ribbing and any interfacings, if required.

3 Lay up the fabric and cut out the T-shirt, following the grain lines very carefully. Fuse any interfacings.

4 Join the shoulder seams and overlock the edges. If a very stretchy fabric is used, insert tape or a strip of self fabric, and cut lengthwise when overlocking to prevent the seam from stretching out. Press the seams towards the back.

5 Join the ribbing ends using 6 mm (¼ in) seams. Fold in half lengthwise, with wrong sides facing, and divide into four equal parts. Mark with pins. Place a pin at the centre front and divide the neck into fourths from that point, marking with pins.

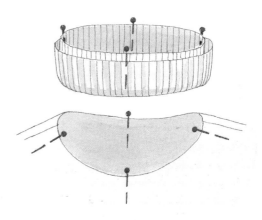

6 Place the ribbing seam at the left shoulder and match the pin markers of the ribbing to those of the neck. With the ribbing on top, stitch a 6 mm (¼ in) seam using an overedge stretch stitch, narrow zigzag or overlock. Stretch the ribbing to fit the garment neck between the pins. Press the seam towards the garment.

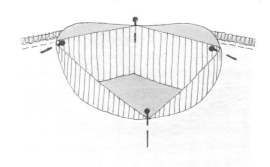

81

7 For a professional-looking finish, bind the back neck, from shoulder to shoulder, encasing the seam allowance in the binding.

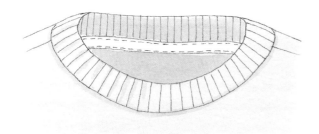

8 Attach pockets at this stage, if required. With right sides facing, match and pin the sleeve to the armhole, aligning the notches. Stitch with the sleeve side up.

9 If top stitching or any other decorative stitching is required around the armhole, overlock the edges, press the seam allowances towards the garment and, with right side up, stitch as required. If no top stitching is required, trim the seams to 6 mm (¼ in) with the over-locker. Press the seams towards the sleeve.

10 With right sides facing, match and pin the underarm seams. Stitch one continuous seam from the hem of the garment to the hem of the sleeve. Trim the seam allowances to 6 mm (¼ in) when over-locking. Overlock and stitch the hems of the sleeves and the body. Trim off all unwanted threads and press.

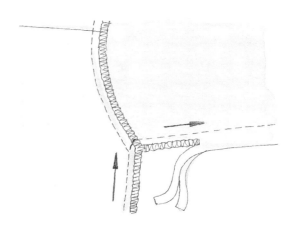

Inside information
- It is very important to cut a knit precisely on the grain line to prevent the side seams from twisting. Knits are circular knitted and if they are finished off-grain, the edges of the fabric might not necessarily be on the grain. Examine the fabric closely to find the true vertical grain.
- Select a ribbing that is similar in weight to the knit. A ribbing that is too heavy or too light looks unprofessional.
- Avoid stretching out the fabric when stitching the hems. Blind stitch if necessary.

82

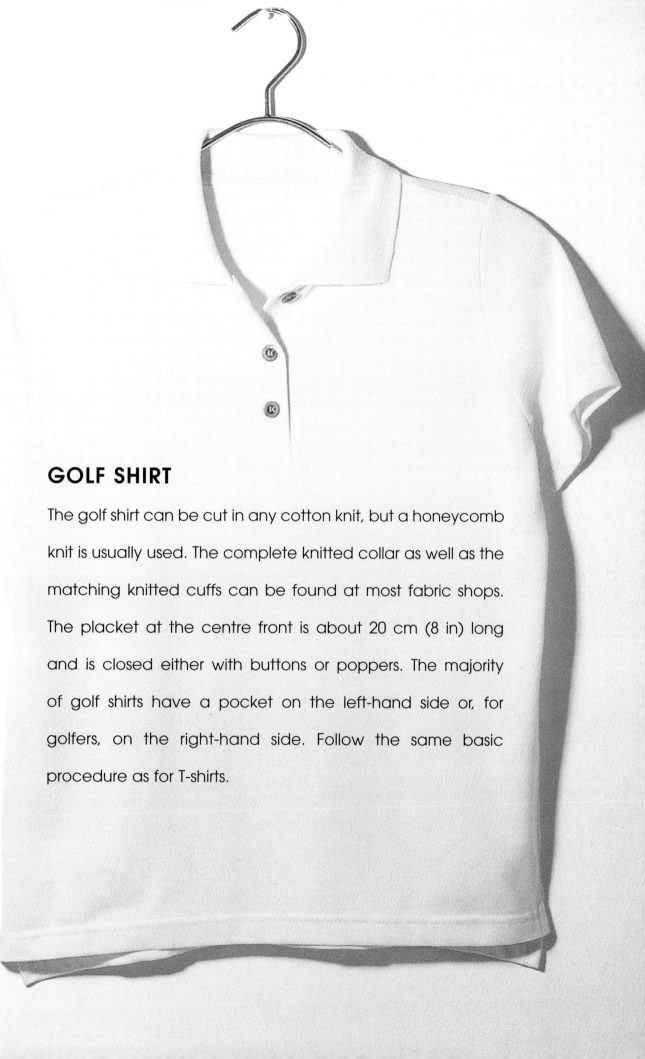

GOLF SHIRT

The golf shirt can be cut in any cotton knit, but a honeycomb knit is usually used. The complete knitted collar as well as the matching knitted cuffs can be found at most fabric shops. The placket at the centre front is about 20 cm (8 in) long and is closed either with buttons or poppers. The majority of golf shirts have a pocket on the left-hand side or, for golfers, on the right-hand side. Follow the same basic procedure as for T-shirts.

1 Select a suitable golf-shirt pattern and pin-fit before cutting to check whether any adjustments are necessary (see pages 41–65).

2 Select the relevant fabric and interfacings for the centre-front plackets.

3 Lay up the fabric and cut out the golf shirt following the grain lines very carefully. Fuse the interfacings.

4 Reinforce the placket opening by stay stitching 1 cm (⅜ in) away from the slit all round. Slash to within 1 cm (⅜ in) of the placket bottom and then to the corners.

5 Fold the placket in half lengthwise and press flat. With right sides together, pin one side of each placket to the opening, aligning the edges, and tack if necessary. Stitch the plackets in place, stopping 1 cm (⅜ in) from the bottom edge.

6 Flip the triangular piece at the bottom of the opening and pin to both the placket ends, taking care to keep the right placket over the left one (vice versa for menswear). Stitch across to secure the plackets. Overlock the unattached edges of the placket, and across the bottom edge, turn to the right side and press.

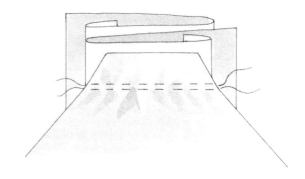

7 Join the shoulder seams and overlock the edges, trimming the seams to 6 mm (¼ in). Insert shoulder tape or similar, if required.

8 Divide the knitted collar and the neck separately into fourths and mark with pins. Turn the placket to the wrong side and match the collar and neck markers, sandwiching the collar between the placket and aligning the edge of the collar with the centre-front notch on the placket.

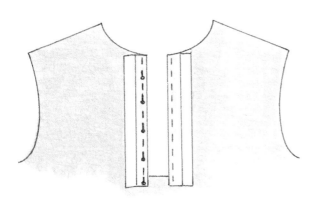

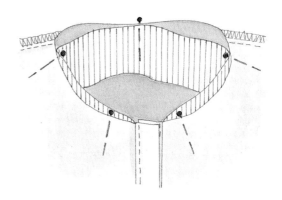

84

9 With the collar on top, start stitching from the folded edge of the placket using an overlock, narrow zigzag or overedge stretch stitch. Maintain a 6 mm (¼ in) seam. Stretch the collar to fit the garment neck between the pins. Press the seam towards the garment. Bind the neck from under the placket, encasing the seam allowance in the binding.

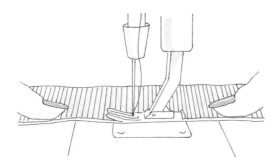

10 Turn the placket to the right side and top stitch or stitch in the seam line, as required.

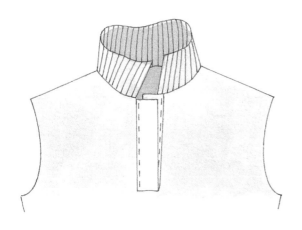

11 If knitted cuffs are required, attach them to the sleeve hem at this stage. Divide the cuff and sleeve hem into fourths and mark with pins. Match these markers, stretch the cuff slightly to fit the sleeve hem and stitch a 6 mm (¼ in) seam using an overedge stretch stitch, narrow zigzag or overlock. With right sides facing, match and pin sleeves to the armhole, aligning the notches. Stitch with the sleeve side up.

12 If pockets are required, attach them at this stage. Hem the pocket, press the seams back, pin in position and stitch down, reinforcing the corners.

13 With right sides facing, match and pin the underarm seams. Stitch one continuous seam from the hem of the garment to the hem of the sleeve. Trim the seam allowances to 6 mm (¼ in) when overlocking. Overlock and stitch the hems of the sleeves and the body. Trim off all unwanted threads and press. (See illustration on page 82.)

85

SWEATSHIRT

Sweatshirts are usually cut in fleece. This fabric could be plain, brushed

on one side for warmth or on both sides as for polar fleece. Other

fancy knits are also suitable as are some wovens,

depending on the effect required. On traditional sweat-

shirts the neck, sleeves and hem are trimmed with ribbing

for added comfort and to keep the warmth in, although

some are just hemmed and others have side slits. The

construction is similar to that of a T-shirt.

1 Follow steps 1 to 9 of the instructions given for the T-shirt (see pages 81–82).

2 With right sides facing, match and pin the under-arm seams. Stitch one continuous seam from the hem of the garment to the hem of the sleeve. Trim the seam allowances to 6 mm (¼ in) when overlocking.

3 Establish the finished width of the cuff and cut twice the width plus 12 mm (½ in) for seams. Measure the length snugly around the wrist and add 12 mm (½ in) for seams. With right sides facing and raw edges together, fold in half widthwise and stitch the seam.

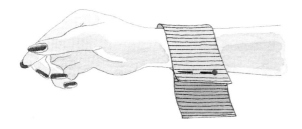

4 With wrong sides facing, fold the cuff in half lengthwise and divide into four equal parts. Mark with pins. Divide the sleeve hem into four equal parts and pin.

5 With right sides together, pin the cuff to the sleeve, matching the seams and aligning the pins. With the cuff side up, stitch the cuff to the sleeve, stretching the cuff to lie flat against the edge of the sleeve.

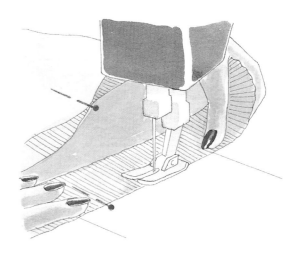

6 Overlock the edges and then press the seam towards the sleeve.

7 Repeat steps 3 to 5 for the hem ribbing, using the same width as for the cuffs. Measure the length of the hem ribbing around the upper hip.

87

SHIRT

Strictly speaking, shirts should be cut in lightweight woven fabrics. The composition of the fabric is not a prerequisite. Natural fibres do crease more easily than polyesters but they have a higher absorbency level. Be sure to correct the tension of the stitches on your sewing machine prior to stitching, as most shirtings can pucker quite easily. Firstly, the collar, cuffs, pockets and button-stands must be prepared before the final assembly of the shirt, as these areas are focal points and require special attention. Following this assembly procedure will result in a professional-looking shirt.

Inside information

- For professional results, be sure to follow the grain lines closely.
- Buttonholes should be neat and clean. Trim all excess threads and protruding bits of interfacing from the buttonholes.
- Use dark interfacing on dark fabrics and white or cream interfacing on light colours. Make sure that both the fabric and the interfacing require the same washing instructions.
- At times it is necessary to fuse both sides of the collar and collar-stand with a lightweight interfacing to achieve a smooth result. This will also prevent the seam allowances from shadowing, a problem which often occurs when using sheer or lightweight fabrics.
- Fuse the cuffs in the same manner as the collar to unify the look. Top stitch close to the edge for a flat, finished effect.
- Press as you sew and at the completion of each operation for a masterly effect.

1 Select the desired shirt pattern and pin-fit before cutting to check for any possible adjustments (see pages 41–65).

2 Select the fabric and interfacing and test that neither shrink nor strike through.

3 Lay up the fabric and cut out the shirt, following the grain lines carefully and pattern matching where necessary. Also, cut out the corresponding interfacings.

4 Fuse the collar, collar-stand, cuffs, button-stands and any pocket facings required. Fold and press the button-stands, cuffs and pockets along their fold lines and press back their seam allowances as required.

5a With right sides facing, pin and stitch the top and under collars together, blunting the corners (see box below). Press the seams flat and trim the edges and the corners.

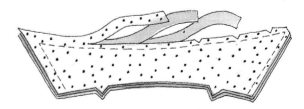

To achieve a precise point on an enclosed corner, sew one stitch diagonally across the corner of a fine fabric, two stitches on a medium-weight and three stitches on bulky fabric, as illustrated. First press the stitches flat, then press the seams open. Turn to the right side and, using an awl, carefully coax out the corner. Press again.

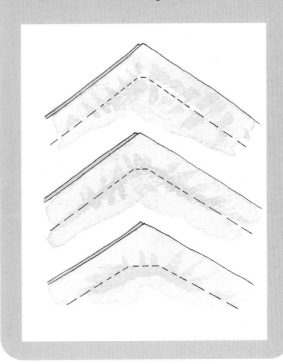

5b Press and turn the collar as suggested in the box on page 89 and top stitch if required. Fold up the collar-stand edge along its neck seam line and towards the wrong side. Press in position, trimming the seam allowance to 6 mm (¼ in).

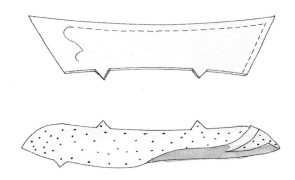

5c With the right side of the under collar facing the right side of the collar-stand, match and pin together along the lower edge of the collar with the stands extending beyond the collar. Place the collar stand facing on top, with right sides facing, align and pin together. Stitch along the seam line, through all the layers, starting and ending 1 cm (⅜ in) from the edge, as illustrated.

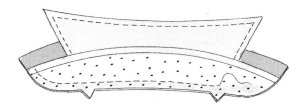

5d Press the seam flat, trim and grade the seams, making the seam of the facing wider, and notch and clip the curved seam allowances. Press the seams open using the tip of the iron. Turn to the right side and use a pressing cloth to press the seam, facing and stand down, away from the collar.

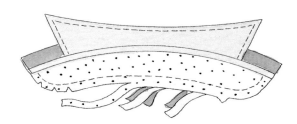

6 Press the one seam allowance of the cuff up towards the fold line. With right sides facing, fold the cuff in half lengthwise and stitch the ends. Press the seam flat and trim the seam allowances, tapering the corners. Turn to the right side and pull out the corners. Roll the facing edges slightly under and press.

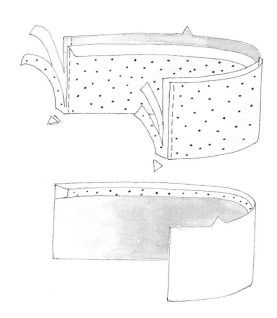

7a Stay stitch any tucks required at the sleeve edge, or ease stitch and draw up the necessary fullness. Bind the slit or prepare the placket as follows in steps 7b to 7j.

7b Fold the overlap placket in half with right sides facing, pin and stitch around the top edge to the matching point at the side. Press the seam flat, trim the seam allowance and clip at the matching point. Turn to the right side, pull out the corners and press flat. Press under the seam allowance along the top edge.

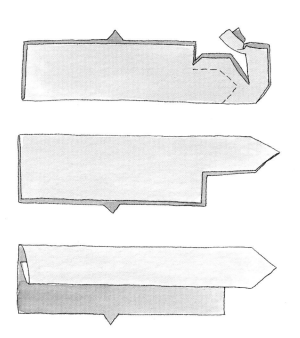

7c Press the seam allowance on the one side of the underlap placket to the wrong side and trim this seam to about half its width.

7d Reinforce the placket opening by stay stitching 1 cm (⅜ in) away from the marked slit all round. Slash to within 1 cm (⅜ in) of the placket top and then to the corners. Determine the front and back edges of the opening.

7e Pin and stitch the right side of the unfolded underlap edge to the wrong side of the back placket edge, aligning the seams. Secure the stitches at the top corner of the placket, then press flat and trim.

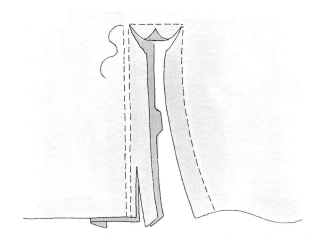

7f Press the seam allowance towards the underlap, fold the underlap towards the right side and pin the folded edge over the stitching line. Edge stitch through all the layers, stop at the corner and secure the stitches.

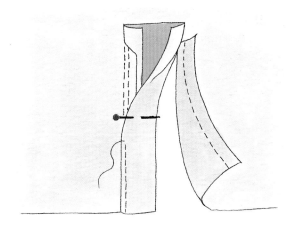

91

7g Flip up the triangular piece at the top of the placket and pin it to the underlap. Stitch across the base of the triangle, securing the stitches at the beginning and at the end. Trim the square corners of the underlap.

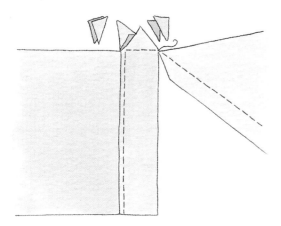

7h Pin and stitch the right side of the unfolded overlap edge to the wrong side of the front placket edge, aligning the seams. Secure the stitches at the top. Press the seam flat, trim the seam allowance to half its width and press again towards the overlap. Bring the folded edge of the overlap to the stitching line and pin in place.

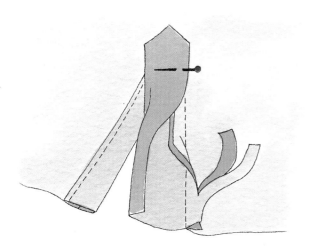

7i Pin the top portion of the overlap to the sleeve, covering the top portion of the underlap and tack down, if necessary. Top stitch along the folded edge of the overlap, but be sure not to catch the underlap in the stitching. Stop stitching at the end of the placket opening, then pull the threads through to the wrong side and knot.

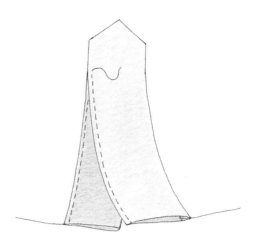

7j Top stitch through all the layers across the overlap, around the pointed end and down to the sleeve edge. Remove any tacking and press.

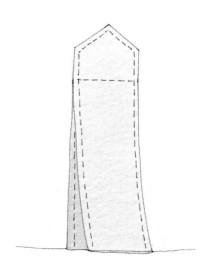

8 Prepare the pockets by folding the facing to the right side along the fold line at the edge of the interfacing and stitch each side on the seam line. Ease stitch rounded corners and mitre square ones. Trim the seam allowances diagonally at the top corners. Turn to the right side, draw up any ease stitching, notching the excess out, and press the pocket flat.

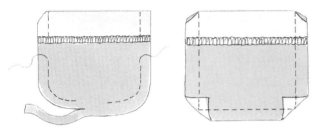

9 Stitch down the front button-stands as required and press flat. Stitch any darts or tucks if necessary. Attach the pockets as required, reinforcing the top corners by bartacking, backstitching or stitching triangles or rectangles.

10a Join the shoulder seams and overlock the edges. If a double yoke is required, follow this method. With right sides together, pin the yoke to the shirt back. Pin the right side of the yoke facing to the wrong side of the shirt back. Stitch all three layers together. Press the yoke and facing upwards, away from the shirt, and into the yoke's permanent position.

10b Top stitch the back yoke seam. Pin the right side of the yoke facing to the wrong side of the front shoulder seams. Stitch and press the seam upwards, towards the facing.

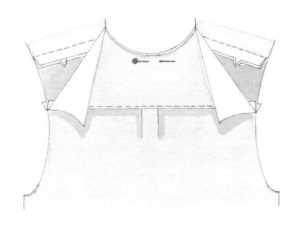

93

10c Press the seam allowance of the yoke shoulder seam under. Match the folded edge to the yoke-facing seam line and top stitch. Stay stitch the neck and shoulder edges together.

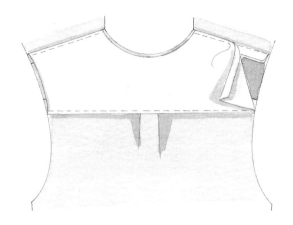

11a Before attaching the collar to the garment, stay stitch the neckline of the garment and clip at intervals. With the right side of the collar-stand facing towards the wrong side of the garment, align and pin together along the neck seam. Stitch along the seam line, securing both ends.

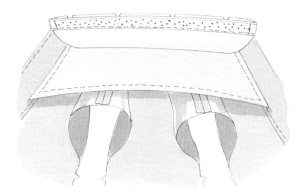

11b Trim, grade and clip the seam allowances where necessary. Press the seam open, then up towards the collar. Align the collar-stand edge with the neck seam line, pin in place and edge stitch carefully along all the edges of the collar-stand, starting and ending on the upper edge at the centre back.

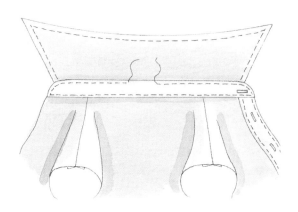

12 If required, ease stitch the sleeve head between the notches and draw up the threads so that they fit those of the armhole. Secure the ends and steam-press along the head to shrink out as much of the puckering as possible. With right sides facing, pin the sleeve to the armhole, aligning the notches. Stitch with the sleeve side up. If top stitching is required, overlock the edges, press the seams towards the garment and top stitch accordingly. Otherwise, trim the seam allowances, overlock the edges and press the seams towards the sleeve.

13 With right sides facing, match and pin the underarm seams. Stitch one continuous seam from the hem of the garment to the hem of the sleeve. Trim the cross seams diagonally, then trim the seam allowances to about 6 mm (¼ in) and overlock the edges.

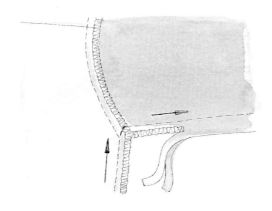

It is unnecessary to trim the seams by hand prior to overlocking. All overlockers have built-in blades that trim and stitch simultaneously.

14a To attach the cuff to the sleeve, first pin the right side of the cuff facing to the wrong side of the sleeve, keeping the cuff ends flush with the underlap and overlap edges of the placket. Distribute any gathers evenly.

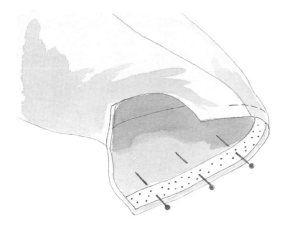

14b Stitch, securing the threads at each end. Press the seam flat, trim the cross-seam allowances and then grade-trim the seams so that the widest is next to the cuff. Pull the cuff down and press the seam allowances towards the cuff.

14c Align the folded edge of the cuff just over the stitching line on the right side of the sleeve. Pin into position and edge stitch. Continue this edge stitching around the entire cuff, if desired. Secure the threads and press.

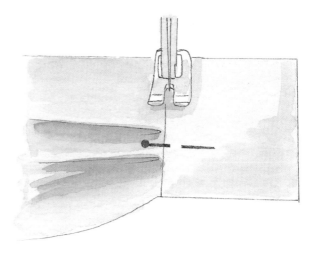

15 For a small hem, suitable on most shirting weights, double turn the hem edge and stitch. For a wider hem, blind stitching may be used if the stitching needs to be concealed.

16 Mark the buttonholes on the centre-front line of the right front button-stand. The one on the collar-stand must be horizontal and those on the garment, vertical. The first buttonhole below the collar should be about 2.5 cm (1 in) down, and the second should be in line with the bust point to prevent the garment from gaping. Space the rest evenly, about 8 cm (3⅛ in) apart, leaving a space of 10–12 cm (4–5 in) between the last buttonhole and the hem. Mark the buttonhole in the middle of the cuff, about 1 cm (⅜ in) from the edge and parallel to the length of the cuff.

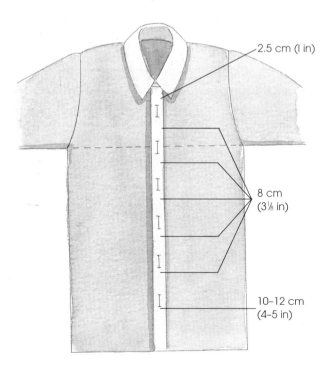

2.5 cm (l in)

8 cm (3⅛ in)

10–12 cm (4–5 in)

Right: Use the same button positioning as depicted above when using a concealed-front button-stand.

17 Mark the button positions on the centre-front line of the left front button-stand, 3 mm (⅛ in) below the top of the buttonhole, as illustrated. Mark the cuff button positions in the same manner.

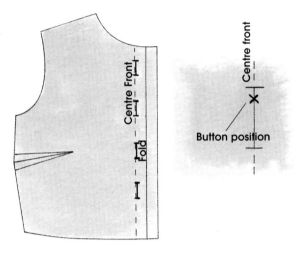

Centre Front

Fold

Centre front

Button position

18 Trim off all unwanted threads and press.

96

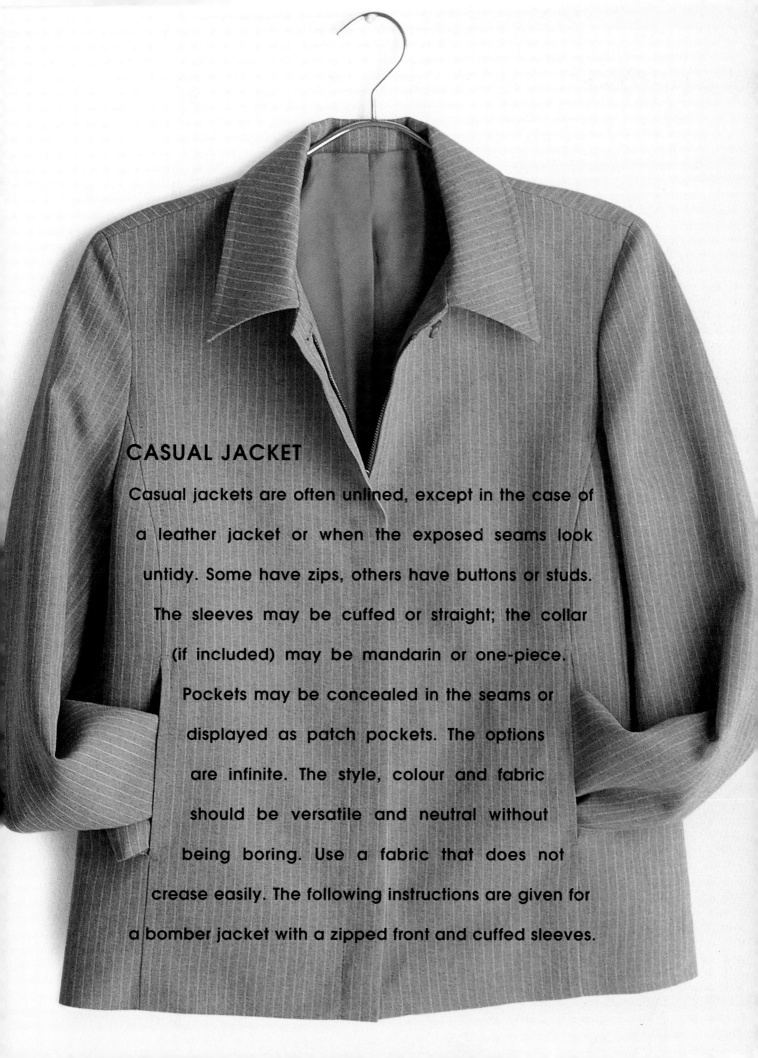

CASUAL JACKET

Casual jackets are often unlined, except in the case of a leather jacket or when the exposed seams look untidy. Some have zips, others have buttons or studs. The sleeves may be cuffed or straight; the collar (if included) may be mandarin or one-piece. Pockets may be concealed in the seams or displayed as patch pockets. The options are infinite. The style, colour and fabric should be versatile and neutral without being boring. Use a fabric that does not crease easily. The following instructions are given for a bomber jacket with a zipped front and cuffed sleeves.

Inside information

- Select a zip that is compatible with the fabric weight. Metal, polyester and nylon teeth are available in various weights.
- Top stitching adds a sporty look and flattens edges, especially on thicker fabrics.
- Use the same interfacing on the collar, cuffs and waistband to maintain uniformity.

1 Select a suitable jacket pattern and pin-fit before cutting to check for possible adjustments (see pages 41–65).

2 Select the appropriate fabric and interfacing and test for compatibility (see Shirt, Inside information on page 89).

3 Lay up the fabric and cut out the jacket, following the grain lines carefully and pattern matching where necessary. Cut the corresponding interfacing.

4 Fuse the collars, cuffs, facings, waistband and pocket flaps and facings. Press back any parts that are folded, for example the waistband, cuffs and pockets.

5 Prepare the collar, cuffs, sleeve placket and pockets of the jacket: follow steps 5 to 8 of the instructions given for the Shirt on pages 89–93. With right sides facing, stitch the pocket flaps, trim the seam allowance to 6 mm (¼ in) and turn to the right side, carefully pushing out the corners. Overlock the raw edges. Press and top stitch, if required.

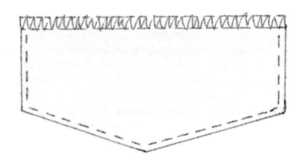

6 Attach the pocket flaps and pockets as required and stitch any darts, tucks or panels, overlocking the raw edges. Stitch the shoulder seams or yokes as instructed for the Shirt on page 93–94, step 10.

Attach the sleeves, close the garment and attach the cuffs, following steps 12 to 14 of the Shirt instructions on pages 94–95.

7 Overlock the outer edge of the facings and one edge of the waistband. With right sides facing, attach the waistband along the raw side only. With right sides facing, attach the bottom edge of the facing to the waistband at the centre front, as illustrated.

8 With right sides together, align the facing and the garment at the neckline, folding the waistband up. Open the zip and sandwich it between the front facing and the garment, with edges aligned, as illustrated. Pin into position and stitch. Turn to the right side and press flat. Top stitch the zip and the free edge of the waistband into position.

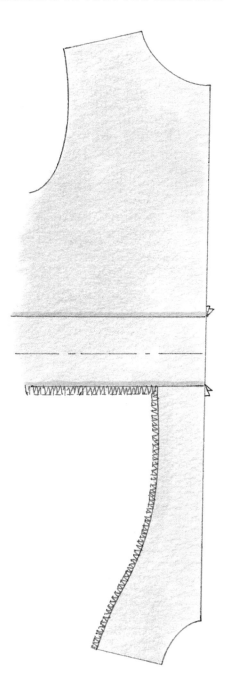

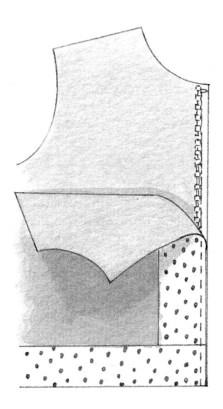

9 Attach the collar following the method for the Shirt on page 94, step 11. Overlock and press after each operation, where necessary.

10 Stitch the buttonholes on the cuffs and attach the buttons, following steps 16 and 17 of the Shirt instructions on page 96. Trim off all unwanted threads and press.

TAILORED JACKET

Tailoring a garment can be a very satisfying experience. Most procedures are not difficult and are used in everyday dressmaking. Custom tailoring is used by professional tailors, but machine and fusible methods are easier and quicker. The correct choice of fabric, lining and interfacing is crucial, as well as accurate cutting, marking, stitching, trimming and pressing. Pin-fitting is also essential and should be done prior to cutting. For your first tailoring project select a fabric that is easy to tailor, preferably nothing with checks, stripes or diagonals.

Inside information

- Natural fibres press and shape well; medium to dark colours conceal inner construction; surface texture can hide stitching imperfections; and medium weaves are flexible and hold their shape.
- Trim and grade the seam allowances to reduce the thickness of layers; bevel trim heavy melton cloth, holding scissors at an angle to skim the edges; shorten stitches around outside curves and notch curves or trim seams to 3 mm (⅛ in).
- Do not overpress: test the iron setting on scrap fabric; use a lower-pause-lift motion instead of sliding the iron; press on the wrong side or use a pressing cloth; do not press over pins or tacking; keep seam lines straight and use shaped pressing equipment when pressing darts and curved seams; tuck a strip of paper under darts to avoid overpressing; and allow the fabric to cool before moving it to prevent it from stretching out of shape.
- To remove the shine from fabric that has been over-pressed, sponge a solution of 1–2 teaspoons of white vinegar to 1 cup of water onto fabric, cover area with a pressing cloth and press lightly. N.B: First test the fabric for colourfastness on a piece of scrap.

- Preshrink fabric to prepare it for the extra steam used when fusing and pressing. Be sure to use compatible linings and interfacings.
- Fuse garment and sleeve hems as well as any vents or pleats. Reinforce the shoulder by fusing a shape on the front from the shoulder to two-thirds of the way down the armhole, just inside the seam line and curved to 12 mm (½ in) from the roll line.
- To prevent the fabric from straining across the shoulder blades and to stabilize the shoulder area, cut the back stay from firmly woven interfacing or muslin: curve a line from the centre back about 23 cm (9 in) below the neck to 7.5 cm (3 in) below the underarm. Pink the lower edge and attach it to the garment back along the neckline, armhole and side.
- If the pattern requires shoulder pads, these should be large enough to cover the entire shoulder area, stopping about 2.5 cm (1 in) from the neckline. The shoulder pad should extend in front to fill the hollow above the bust and should be narrow enough to clear the shoulder blades at the back. Check your pattern to ascertain the correct thickness of the pad.

1 Select a suitable jacket pattern and pin-fit or make up a test garment to ascertain any possible adjustments (see pages 41–65).

2 Select suitable fabric and compatible lining and interfacing (refer to the box above).

3 Lay up the fabric and cut out the jacket, carefully following the grain lines and pattern matching where required. Cut the lining and corresponding interfacing, removing the wedge of interfacing on the dart stitching lines.

4 Fuse the fronts, collar, facings, pocket openings, pockets, sleeve and garment hems and any other sections requiring support. Press back any fold lines and seam allowances where required.

5 Stitch any darts and attach any patch pockets (see page 93). Sew single or double welt pockets and bound buttonholes at this stage, if required (refer to the boxes on pages 102–105).

Bound buttonholes

This simple method can also be used to make double welt pockets and requires only one strip of fabric per buttonhole. To strengthen the buttonhole, draw wool or soft cord into the welts before the triangular ends are stitched together, as illustrated.

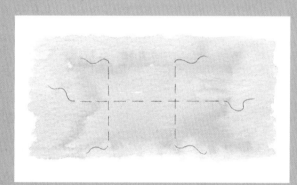

1 Before constructing the buttonholes, mark both ends and the centre of each one accurately by machine tacking.

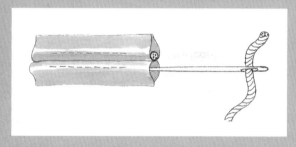

2 Cut a strip 2.5 cm (1 in) wide and as long as required, remembering to add an extra 2.5 cm (1 in) per buttonhole. Fuse only if the fabric frays. Cut the strip into equal lengths per buttonhole.

3 With wrong sides together, fold and press the patch in half lengthwise, marking the centre with a crease. With right sides together, centre the crease of the patch directly over the buttonhole markings and machine tack.

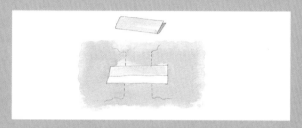

4 Fold and press the long raw edges of the patch to meet at the centre tacking line. Use a fine stitch length, stitch through the exact centre of each half of the patch, start and stop exactly on the markings for the ends of the buttonholes.

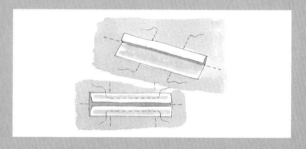

5 Do not backstitch, but pull the threads to the wrong side and tie. Remove the tacking threads and press. Cut through the centre of the patch to form two welts, taking care not to cut through the garment fabric underneath. Turn to the wrong side, cut along the centre line and then into each corner, just short of the stitching, as illustrated.

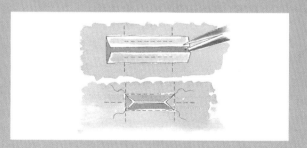

6 Carefully push the welts through the opening to the wrong side and adjust them to square off the corners. Tack the welts together diagonally by hand. Press.

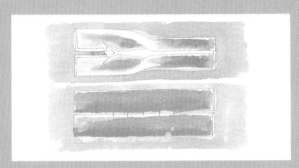

7 Place the garment on the machine, with right side up, and fold back the fabric just enough to expose one of the triangular buttonhole ends. Stitch back and forth along this line to secure it to the welts. Repeat at the other end.

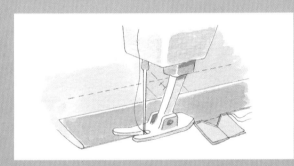

8 Remove any remaining tacking threads, trim the welt ends to 6 mm (¼ in) and press them with the tip of the iron.

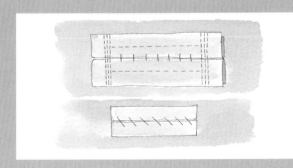

9 When the front facing is attached to the garment, press the facing flat and then secure it in position by pinning around each buttonhole. Insert a pin at each corner of the buttonhole through to the facing side.

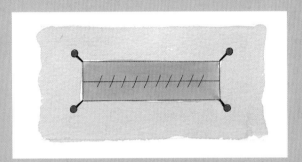

10 Turn to the facing side and cut along the centre of this pinned area and then into each corner, just short of the pins. Remove the pins.

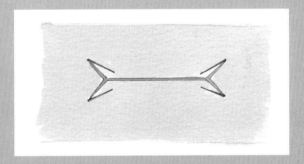

11 Carefully turn back the edges on all four sides and align with the buttonhole. Slip stitch the facing to the back of the buttonhole.

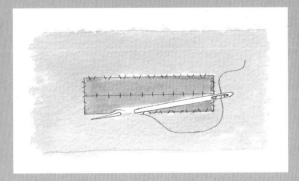

SINGLE WELT POCKET

1 Fuse the welt and a narrow strip at the pocket opening, using the appropriate interfacing. Fold the welt in half lengthwise, with right sides facing, and pin and stitch the ends. Trim the seams and the corners and turn to the right side. Press.

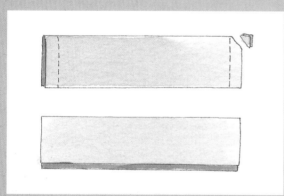

2 Mark the welt's window frame, as indicated on your pattern, as well as the centre line. Cut along this centre line, and then into each corner, stopping just short of the stitching.

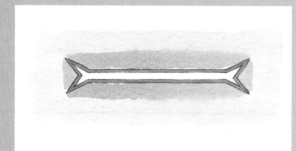

3 With right sides facing and raw edges together, pin and stitch the welt to the pocket facing. With the wrong side of the garment facing the right side of the pocket facing, slide the welt through the window frame, aligning the raw edges of the welt/facing seam with the bottom edge of the window frame.

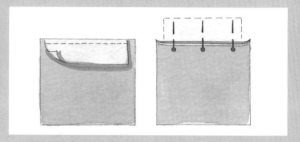

4 Do not stitch beyond the ends of the frame. Pin and stitch the pocket to the top edge of the window frame.

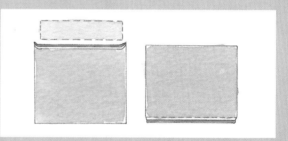

5 With the garment side up, flip back enough to expose the triangular ends. Stitch back and forth across the triangle and stitch one continuous seam, joining the pocket facing to the pocket. Repeat on the other side. Overlock the pocket edges. Reinforce the ends of the welts with edge stitching or slip stitch by hand.

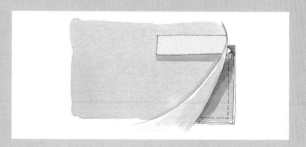

DOUBLE WELT POCKET

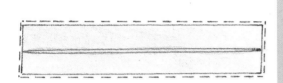

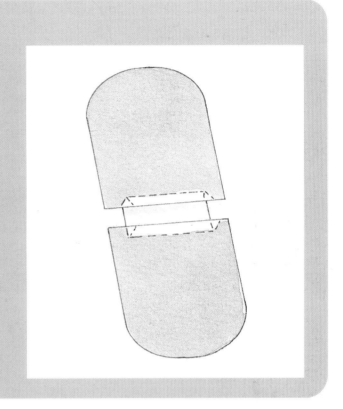

1 Follow the instructions for the Bound Buttonhole (steps 1 to 4, page 102), positioning the pocket and facing on top of the strip, with the open ends meeting at the centre line. If a pocket flap is required, sandwich the finished flap between the strip and the pocket before stitching.

2 Continue through to step 7 of the Bound Buttonhole instructions, pushing the welts and pocket pieces through the opening. Now follow step 5 of the Single Welt Pocket (opposite) to finish the pocket.

6 Join the shoulder seams of the garment as well as the facings. Stay stitch the neck seam line on the jacket and the facing. Clip the seam allowances where necessary.

7 Match the notches of the under collar to the garment, pin in place and stitch, starting and ending at the lapel notches. Clip to these notches, press the seam open and trim the excess seam allowance to 6 mm (¼ in) to reduce bulk.

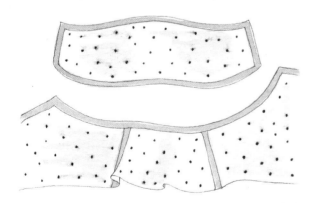

8 Repeat this procedure when attaching the top collar to the facing. Trim the seam allowances to 1 cm (⅜ in), slightly wider than those of the under collar, and press as before.

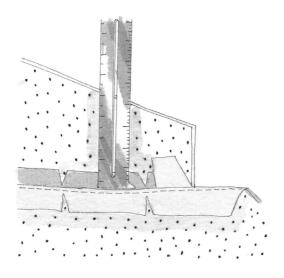

9 Pin the top collar/facing section to the under collar/jacket section. Pin through the seams at the collar notches, making sure that the seams line up precisely. Trim the excess fabric of the collar seam allowance to the stitching line on the top and under the collar.

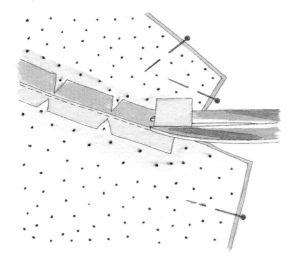

10 Stitch the seam, starting at the bottom of the jacket edge. Take one or two short diagonal stitches across the lapel point. Stitch from the lapel point to the collar point, holding the seam straight to ensure that the notches match on both sides of the jacket collar. Finish stitching the seam, using the same technique on the other side.

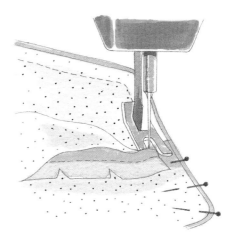

11 Press the seams open using the tip of the iron. Diagonally trim the corners close to the stitching. Trim the seam allowances of the under collar/jacket to 6 mm (¼ in) and those of the top collar/facing to 1 cm (⅜ in), continuing to the lapel roll line notch. Clip this notch and continue trimming the seam allowances: the jacket front to 1 cm (⅜ in) and the facing to 6 mm (¼ in). Press the seam open and turn to the right side.

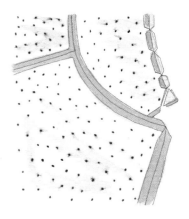

106

12 Stitch the top and under collar seams together. If the seams do not line up exactly because of the bulk of the fabric, tack the seams where they meet.

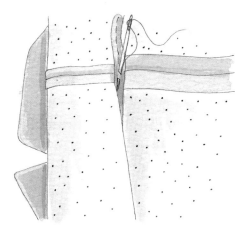

13 Press the collar and lapels from the underside. Roll the seam towards the underside of the collar and lapels, stopping about 2.5 cm (1 in) from the end of the roll line. Press and pound the edges with a tailor's clapper (block of wood) to create a crisp edge. Press the jacket front below the roll line from the inside so that the seams roll towards the jacket facing.

14 If required, top stitch on the right side of the jacket, starting at the one lower edge. Stop at the roll line and pull the threads through to the facing side, burying the ends between the facing and the garment.

15 Continue on the right side of the lapel, overlapping the first two stitches at the start. At the collar notch, pivot and then stitch up to the notch edge. Pivot and 'stitch in the ditch' to the top stitching line of the collar. Pivot and stitch around the collar to the other notch. Repeat at the second notch, breaking the top stitching at the roll line on the other side. Pull the threads through as before and continue stitching on the jacket side to the lower edge.

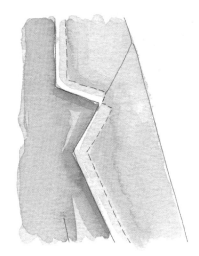

107

16 Stitch the side seams of the jacket and the seams of the sleeves. Ease stitch the sleeve head and draw up the thread so that the notches of the sleeve and armhole match. Secure the ends, shrink out the excess with a steam iron and then pin the sleeve back into the armhole.

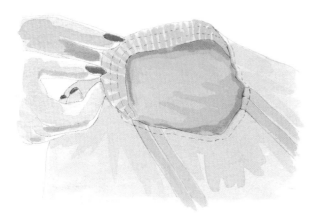

17 Stitch and press only the sleeve-head seam allowance, up to 3 mm (⅛ in) beyond the seam line into the head. This will prevent the head from flattening. Do not press the underarm. Trim the underarm seams to 6 mm (¼ in).

18 Add a sleeve pad to support the sleeve head and prevent the seam allowance from showing on the right side. Cut a bias strip of lamb's wool, heavy flannel or fleecy non-woven fabric, 5 x 23 cm (2 x 9 in). Fold 1.5 cm (⅝ in) from one long edge and align the folded edge with the sleeve-head seam line, so that the wider side faces the sleeve. Slip stitch the folded edge to the sleeve seam.

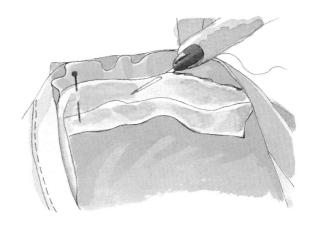

19 Pin a shoulder pad into the garment so that it extends 12 mm (½ in) beyond the seam line. Fit the jacket and adjust the pad, if necessary. Attach to the shoulder seam by hand, using loose stitches, and tack the lower edge of the pad to the armhole seam. Do not stitch through all the layers of the pad.

20 Hem the sleeves and the jacket using a catch stitch or blind stitch. Should the jacket be unlined, bind the hem edges or turn the edges back and flat stitch before blind stitching the hems.

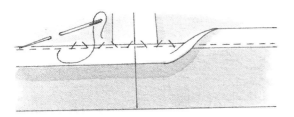

21 Stitch the lining sections together, including the sleeves. Reinforce the armhole seam with two rows of stitching. Fold and machine tack the centre back pleat at the top and bottom of the lining. Stay stitch the neckline, sleeve and bottom edge of the lining, and clip the seams at the neck.

22 With right sides together, stitch the lining to the jacket, starting and ending double the hem depth away from the bottom edge. Clip the seams at the curves and press the seams as they are stitched.

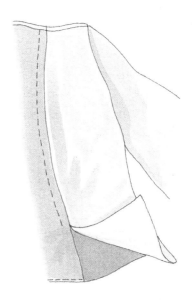

23 Match the seam allowances of the lining and the jacket at the shoulder and the under-arm seams, and then tack in place. Lightly press the facing/lining seam allowances towards the lining, using a pressing cloth.

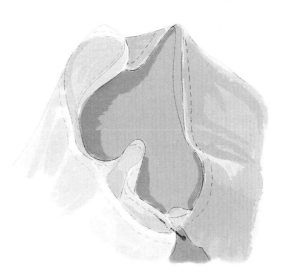

24 Trim the raw edges of the lining to 1.5 cm (⅝ in) below the finished jacket edge. If the hem needs easing, ease stitch 1 cm (⅜ in) from that edge. Turn back the lining by about 2.5 cm (1 in) so that the fold is 1 cm (⅜ in) from the jacket edge. Pin the lining to the jacket, placing the pins 1 cm (⅜ in) above and parallel to the fold.

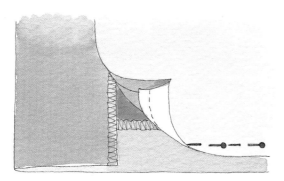

25 Fold the lining back along the pinned line and slip stitch it to the garment hem, catching the underlayer of the lining only. Remove the pins and press the lining fold lightly. Slip stitch the remaining lining edges to the facing. Hem the sleeve in the same manner.

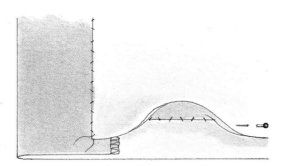

26 If bound buttonholes have been made, follow steps 9 to 11 from the box on bound buttonholes (pages 102–103), to complete the back of these buttonholes. Otherwise carefully mark and make machine buttonholes. Mark the buttons accordingly and attach. Finally, press the jacket lightly.

Inside information

- Buttons add distinction to a tailored jacket. They should be simple, high-quality buttons such as bone, mother-of-pearl, tortoiseshell or brass. They must have a shank to lift the button away from the thickness of the fabric and to avoid strain on the buttonhole. Make a thread shank for sew-through buttons when stitching them onto the garment.
- Buttonholes should be expertly sewn. Bound buttonholes take time to perfect. Master the technique and make several samples to check the finished length before attempting them on the garment. It is preferable to use cord machine-worked buttonholes to add a professional finish.

TROUSERS

The key to an elegant pair of trousers is to select the most appropriate fabric in the correct weight for the chosen style, and to cut the panels on the grain line. Special care must be taken when stitching the fly, pockets, pleats and waistband. Consult the section on Trouser Adjustments on pages 71–77 before advancing to the cutting stage. The same procedures can be followed for pleated trousers, jeans and shorts. The following instructions are for trousers with closed seams. For open seams, overlock the edges prior to assembling the panels, and stitch and press open the seams before continuing.

Inside information

- Pin-fitting is not a suitable method for trousers. It will only be necessary to make a new fitting shell when your figure changes substantially.
- Try to merge one of the waist tucks with the crease line and only press down above the crotch.
- Interface all pocket openings to prevent them from stretching out. The length of the opening on a hip pocket should extend the side seam by about 1 cm (⅜ in). This prevents the opening from pulling tightly across the hip.
- Match the pattern and fabric grain lines accurately to prevent the side seams from twisting.

1 Select a suitable pattern and make up a trial garment to work out the initial adjustments. This task will streamline future projects.

2 Select an appropriate fabric and test various interfacings to ascertain compatible qualities suitable for the waistband and pockets.

3 Lay up the fabric and cut out the trousers, following the grain lines very carefully. Cut the interfacings accordingly.

4 Fuse the interfacings on the waistband and pockets, taking note of the guidelines given by the manufacturer.

5 Stitch any back darts, securing the ends. Pin any tucks in position and reinforce by stitching across the top just outside the seam line. For jeans, attach any yokes and top stitch.

(Ignore step 6 if no pockets are required)

6a With right sides facing, pin and stitch the pocket facing to the garment along the opening edge of the pocket. Press flat, then trim the seams, clipping or notching out the curves.

6b Press the seam open, then press both towards the facing. Understitch the facing close to the seam line, through all the layers. Turn the facing towards the inside and press. Top stitch, if required.

6c With right sides together, pin and stitch the pocket to the facing. Press and overlock the edges. Secure the pocket to the front along the waist and side seam, by stitching just outside the seam line.

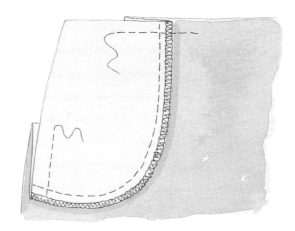

7a With right sides together, stitch the fly facing to the right front. Overlock the edges of this facing, the right front crotch and the left front crotch.

112

7b Press the seam flat, so that the edges face the garment, and align the zip, facing down, with the seam line. Pin in place and, using the zip foot, stitch from the top downwards, close to the teeth.

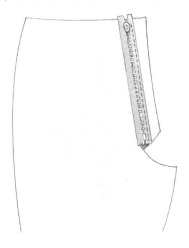

7c Stitch the bottom seam of the placket, then turn to the right side and press. Overlock the vertical edge of the placket.

7d First place the placket with the overlocked edge to the right-hand side, then position the other side of the zip, facing upwards, on top of the placket. Lastly, position the left front, right-side down, on top of the zip. Ensure that all the edges are aligned. Pin in place and stitch.

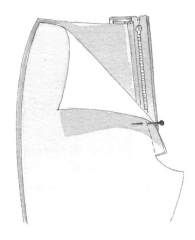

7e Turn over and stitch the crotch from the bottom at the inside leg to just beyond the seam line of the fly and then backstitch.

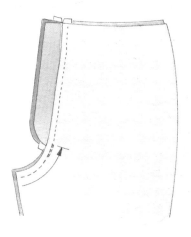

7f Turn the garment to the right side, fold the fly back on the seam line and press. Secure the fly with pins, keeping the placket aside to prevent it from being caught in the stitching. Mark the fly with tailor's chalk and top stitch. Reinforce the bottom of the fly, vertically, with a bartack.

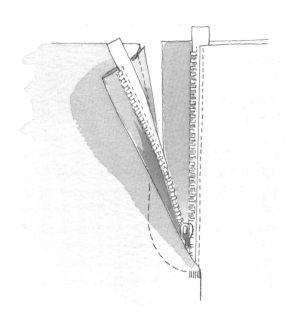

113

8 Stitch the back crotch seam, overlock the edges, press and top stitch, if required. Join the side seams, aligning the notches, overlock the edges, press and top stitch, if required.

9 Join the inside leg seam, aligning the notches and the crotch seams, stitching continuously from the hem of the one leg to the hem of the other leg. Overlock the edges and press.

10 Make the belt loops, if required. Attach them to the waistline at the appropriate positions.

11 With right sides facing, fold the waistband in half lengthwise and stitch across both ends. Trim the corners, turn to the right side and press. Stay stitch the waistline seam and attach the waistband to the trousers. Stitch the belt loops in place and bartack to secure.

12 Hem the trousers either by hand or blind stitch by machine. Stitch the buttonhole and button in place. Press the crease, aligning the side seams.

Right: *Pleated trousers will always be regarded as a classic.*

TRACKSUIT PANTS

Although it is not essential to use a knitted fabric

for tracksuit pants, be sure to use a quality fabric

that does not stretch out or bag at the knee. Certain

wovens are also suitable and may be lined for added

warmth. Most tracksuit pants are elasticated at the ankle

and very few have ribbed cuffs. If required, select a ribbing

that contains a percentage of Lycra which will provide more

stability to the cuffs. The waistband, is also elasticated for further

comfort and ease. These pants are quick and easy to make.

1 Select a suitable pattern for tracksuit pants and adjust the fit as required (see Trouser Adjustments on pages 71–77).

2 Select the appropriate fabric (and ribbing, if required), lay it up and cut out the pants strictly according to the grain lines.

3 Stitch the front and back crotch seams and overlock the edges. Press. Join the side seams, aligning the notches, and overlock the edges. Join the inside leg seam, aligning the notches and crotch seams, stitching continuously from the hem on the one leg to the hem on the other leg. Overlock the edges and press. For lined pants, repeat this step, using the lining.

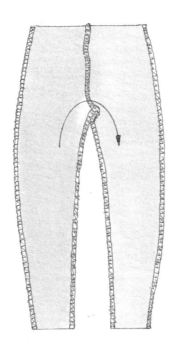

4 Overlock the waist and hem edges. For lined pants, overlock the lining together with the fabric at the waist and hem edges and continue as one piece of fabric. Fold the fabric towards the inside along the marked hemlines and stitch the casings at the waist and hem, leaving a small opening through which to thread the elastic.

5 Measure the elastic snugly around the waist and ankles, allowing 1–2 cm (⅜–¾ in) for the overlap. Cut and, using a bodkin or safety pin, thread the elastic through the casing, taking care not to twist the elastic. Overlap the ends and stitch, as illustrated. Stitch the opening closed.

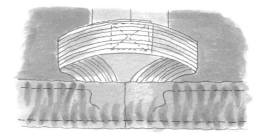

6 For ribbed cuffs, establish the width of the cuffs adding 12 mm (½ in) for seams. Measure the length snugly around the ankle, adding 12 mm (½ in) for seams.

7 With right sides facing and raw edges together, fold the cuff in half widthwise and stitch the seam. With wrong sides facing, fold the cuff in half lengthwise and divide into four equal parts. Mark with pins. Divide the leg into four equal parts at the hem and pin.

8 With right sides together, pin the cuff to the leg, matching the seams and aligning the pins. With the cuff side up, stitch the cuff to the leg, stretching the cuff to lie flat against the edge of the leg. Overlock the edges and press the seam towards the leg.

116

LINED SKIRT

Lining a skirt will add more body to the garment, resulting in a professional appearance. If a lining pattern is not included with your skirt pattern, simply use the skirt pattern and adjust the length so that it finishes about 2.5 cm (1 in) above the skirt hem. The classic pencil skirt with a centre-back vent is a suitable style for medium- to heavyweight fabrics. Pleated skirts require a certain percentage of polyester in the fabric so that the pleats can be permanently retained. Medium-weight fabrics such as linen, gabardine and tightly woven wools are best. Unpressed pleats and released tucks soften the lines of a skirt and require fluid fabrics such as knits, challis and crepe de Chine.

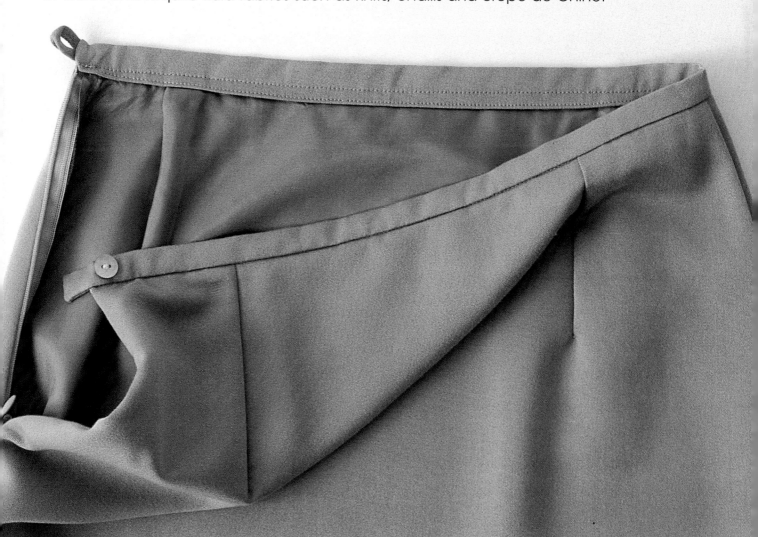

Inside information

- Allow bias-cut skirts about a fortnight to stretch out before finally trimming the hem straight.
- Straight-skirt hems should not be wider than 5 cm (2 in), but full-skirt hems may be anything from 2.5 cm (1 in) to as narrow as a rolled hem.
- Do not attach the lining to the skirt hem. A free-hanging slip lining facilitates ironing and will not bag if the fabric stretches slightly.
- Unless the fabric frays badly, it is not necessary to overlock the edges of a lined skirt.
- Permanent pleats are best done professionally. Most commercial pleaters will pleat for the individual, alternatively, ask your local dry-cleaner.
- Top stitching pleats from the waist to the hips will have a slimming effect.
- When pressing pleats, place strips of brown paper under each pleat to prevent a strike-through reaction.

1 Select a suitable pattern and pin-fit to check for any possible adjustments (see pages 66–70).

2 Select an appropriate fabric and lining, and test the waistband for a compatible interfacing.

3 Lay up the fabric and cut out the skirt, following the grain lines carefully and pattern matching where necessary. Also cut the lining according to the grain lines and then cut the corresponding interfacing.

4 Fuse the waistband and any other pieces requiring interfacing. Press back along the fold line.

5 Stitch any darts, tucks or gathers at the waist and draw up where necessary. Stitch any pockets as previously instructed on page 112, step 6. For skirts requiring permanent pleating, hem at this stage.

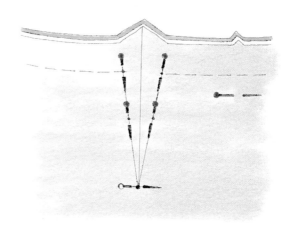

6 Stitch the seam requiring a zip, leaving an opening for the zip. Fold the seam allowances under and press.

118

7 With the right side of the garment facing up and the zip open, place the zip face down on the skirt, with the teeth on the pressed seam line. Pin in position and stitch from the bottom to the top. Close the zip and fold the seam allowance back.

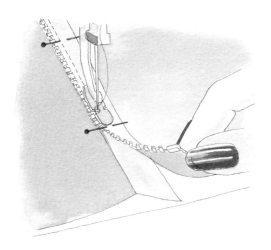

8 Position the pressed seam allowance on the free side of the zip so that the fold overlaps the teeth. Pin or glue into place and stitch across the bottom and up the side, pivoting at the corner and using a guide for the top stitching. Pull the threads through to the wrong side and secure.

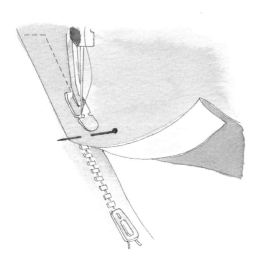

9 Attach any pockets and stitch the remaining seams, aligning the notches. Press the seams.

10a Stitch the darts or tucks on the lining and close the seams, except for the zip opening.

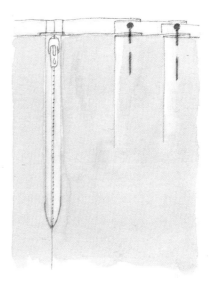

10b For a gathered waist, attach the lining to the skirt at the waist just outside the stitch line and gather the two simultaneously.

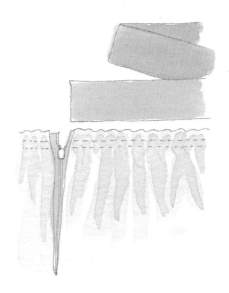

11 Turn to the wrong side and attach the lining to the zip tape by machine, or slip stitch on the right side by hand. Stay stitch the skirt and the lining together at the waist.

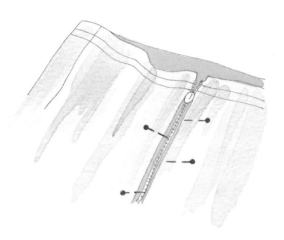

12 Fold the waistband in half lengthwise, with right sides facing, and stitch across both ends. Trim the seam allowances, turn to the right side and push out the corners. Press.

13 With right sides together, pin the waistband to the garment edge, carefully matching all the notches. Ensure that the left-back edge of the waistband is flush with the edge of the zip, and that the underlap is on the right-back side.

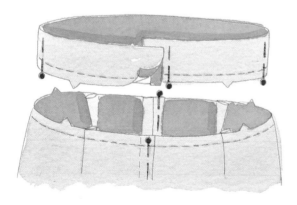

14 Stitch, easing the skirt if necessary, but be sure not to allow any tucks to form. Press, grade, trim and clip the seam.

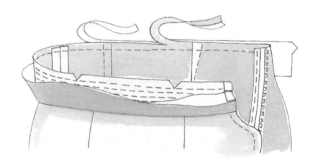

15 Turn to the right side and press the seam up towards the waistband. Fold up this seam allowance at the underlap and edge stitch the lower edge of the waistband, with right side up, catching the inside waistband in the seam. Alternatively, slip stitch by hand or 'stitch in the ditch'.

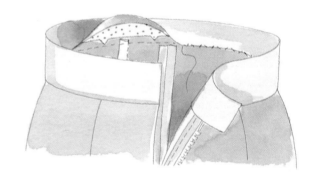

16 Blind stitch the hem, stitch the lining by machine and press. Attach the lining to the vent by machine or stitch by hand. Mark and stitch the buttonhole and attach the button.

DRESS

Most dresses are quite simple to assemble, but I've chosen the princess line to discuss because of its universal appeal and timeless shape. When sewing a shirtwaister, follow the instructions for a shirt and a skirt, joining the two at the waist. Whether the waists are raised or dropped, the same procedure applies. For a simple chemise, follow the same course as for a T-shirt. Medium- to lightweight fabrics such as crepe, gabardine, wool and linen are best, although most fabrics would be suitable.

Inside information

- Unless the lining of a dress is attached to neck and armhole facings, be sure to cut the lining 3 mm (⅛ in) smaller than the dress and understitch the seams to prevent it from rolling to the right side.
- Follow the grain lines carefully, especially on a panelled dress. This will dramatically influence the balance and fall of the dress.
- Hems on flared dresses should be narrow to prevent roping, but they may be wider on straight styles.

1 Select the appropriate pattern for your dress and pin-fit to check for any possible adjustments (see pages 41–70).

2 Select a suitable fabric, taking into account whether the dress is to be worn at night or during the day, or whether it needs to be suitable for both occasions. Select a compatible lining and interfacing, if required.

3 Lay up the fabric and cut out the dress, as well as the linings and interfacings where applicable.

4 Fuse any facings and collars if required. Join the centre-back seam or other seam requiring a zip and, for a lapped zip, attach as instructed for Skirts on pages 118–120.

5 For a centred zip, machine tack the opening and press the seam open. Centre the zip on this seam, pin or glue into position and top stitch down, using a zipper foot. Stitch both sides in the same direction to avoid puckering.

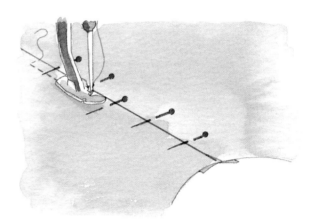

6 With right sides facing, join the front and back panels and the side seams, carefully aligning the notches. Join the underarms of the facing and stay stitch the neckline of the dress and facing. Pin a narrow tuck in the front and back shoulders of the dress: this will prevent the facing seams from showing.

7 Pin the facing to the dress around the armholes and the front and back neckline. Start and end stitching about 1 cm (⅜ in) away from the shoulder edges. Trim, grade and clip the seam allowances.

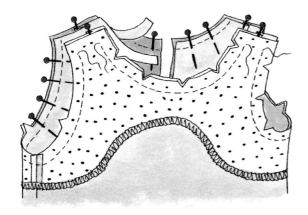

8 With the wrong side up, lightly press the seam allowances towards the facing. Turn the facing to the inside and, with the facing side up, understitch close to the seam line where possible. Press.

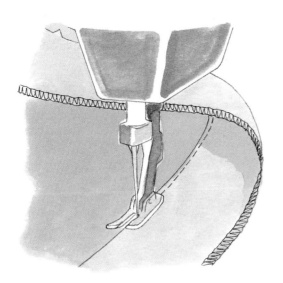

9 Release the tucks at the shoulders. With the neck and armhole seam allowances folded back and the facing folded out of the way, stitch the shoulder seams of the dress. Press the seams, first flat and then open, and push through the opening.

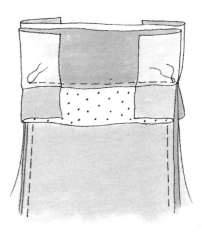

10 Trim the facing seam allowance to 6 mm (¼ in), turn under and then slip stitch by hand. Tack the facings down or 'stitch in the ditch' at all the strategic seams.

11 If lined, join the lining seams, leaving the opening for the zip, and press all seams open. With right sides facing, attach the lining to the facing and press so that the facing faces down. Slip stitch the lining to the zip, blind stitch the dress and hem the lining. Trim off all unwanted threads and press.

chapter five

Final touches

Accessories can make or mar an outfit. They should fit the occasion and enhance rather than overpower the chosen garment. During the 1950s, mismatched shoes, bags, belts and gloves were simply unacceptable. Black and brown were sensible colours to wear, colourful accessories were decidedly risqué! Today black, brown and navy still remain classic colours for shoes, bags and belts, but cream, white and gold have been added to the list.

The key to a total, individual look is through the clever and creative use of accessories. They can perform diverse tasks, dressing an outfit up or down, or even updating a garment to keep up with current trends. It is certainly more economical to purchase accessories than to replace your existing wardrobe.

Shoes

The most obvious way to dress an outfit up or down is by changing the shoes. They should never be an afterthought as they dictate the mood almost instantaneously. Quality is essential. Leather and suede may be expensive, but it is better to buy one good pair of shoes than several cheap immitations. Although shoe design changes from season to season, you simply cannot go wrong with a pair of court shoes, a must for every classic wardrobe. Other suitable styles include stacked heels and high vamps; a pair of brogues or loafers for casual wear that will suffice for summer and winter alike; strappy sandals in metallic calfskin; novelty evening pumps in satin, velvet, snakeskin or patent leather; and a pair of comfortable sneakers. Make sure that each pair is versatile enough to be worn for more than one occasion.

Hosiery

Stockings and pantihose, or tights, are available in various types and brands. However, it is definitely worth spending a little extra for quality. Colour, texture and denier require careful consideration. Natural skin tones are ideal for daytime, while dark charcoal or black looks very elegant at night. Fine-knit tights are smoother to the touch, more uniform in colour and generally have a better appearance than micromesh, but they are more expensive. Sheer tights range from 30 to seven denier, the finest being the lowest number. They are more costly but certainly more elegant than the thicker deniers. Be sure to wear tights with sheer toes and heels when wearing them with sandals. Knee-high stockings should only be worn under trousers.

Socks are best worn with loafers, sneakers or similar casual shoes. Select a colour that is subtle and tones in with your shoes and trousers. Even though natural fibres such as cotton, wool and silk are more costly, they are far superior to polyester or nylon. Cotton socks too have natural absorbency, making them ideal to wear when playing sport.

Belts

Belts are essential to every wardrobe. They should be special enough to be the focal point of an outfit. Metallic finishes, suede sashes or elaborate cowboy belts with silver buckles come to mind here. Crocodile, snake-, lizard, elephant and other skins are very expensive, but good imitations are readily available and can be substituted. Simple, narrow belts in leather and suede with square buckles add an unobtrusive finish and work well with all clothes. A wide patent leather belt with a simple buckle can look very elegant. Belts can be rigid or soft, in skin or fabric, and they can be adapted to suit any occasion.

Styles and widths change from season to season, but a simple and uncluttered design in a classic colour such as black, brown or navy is the most versatile.

Bags

It is a waste of money buying a bag to match each outfit or each pair of shoes – one or two should be sufficient. Neutral shades are infallible and smaller bags are more versatile than large ones. Alternatively, a small bag or purse can be used in conjunction with a large one to take you from day to evening.

The variety of bags available today is endless, ranging from leather, suede and skins such as snake and buffalo, to fabrics such as canvas, tapestry, satin and even straw. Styles also vary according to their use: leather shoulder bags are practical for everyday use; clutch bags are dressier and good for evening wear; backpacks allow freedom of movement; and holdalls provide space. A classic style in a neutral colour, however, will have more mileage.

Jewellery

Earrings, necklaces, chains, brooches, watches, bracelets and rings must be worn with discretion. They need not be matching sets but they must be compatible. You can't go wrong with a good string of pearls, a gold chain, a couple of gold or silver bracelets, simple studs and a classic watch in your wardrobe. They can be worn with traditional and modern classics alike.

A mental division separates real and fake jewellery, but there are no hard and fast rules against mixing the two. And real does not necessarily mean expensive. A slim gold or silver chain need not cost more than a fake necklace, but it will always look good.

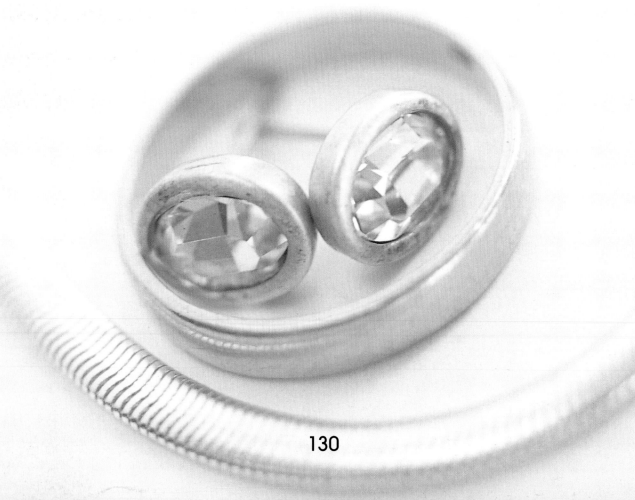

Scarves

Scarves are very adaptable. Depending on the fabric and size, a scarf can be a winter shawl, a bandana or even a sarong; a neckline can be softened or colour added to an outfit. Experiment in front of a mirror to learn how to tie a scarf effortlessly – a hard knot or scarf ring looks too deliberate. Silk scarves are slippery and difficult to handle, whereas wool, cotton and lace scarves are easier to control. At times it is better to pin down a scarf with a suitable brooch, rather than knot or tie it. Large woollen scarves can be worn loosely over the shoulder, mufflers and cobweb-mohair scarves can be twisted and knotted at the neck, and square-shaped scarves can be folded into oblongs for various applications.

Clever combinations

Creative use of accessories and various items of clothing can make the most basic wardrobe seem limitless. Combined or isolated textures have varied effects; the seasons can be bridged with astute mingling; and transformations can be created using varying tones of one colour or a single tone throughout the ensemble.

The following pages show examples of how you can transform the look to suit the occasion without having to change your entire outfit. A simple exchange of a cardigan for a tailored jacket can alter the look from casual to corporate, and paring down a style can be as effective as dressing it up with a piece of jewellery.

Modern and traditional classics can be successfully combined to achieve a certain look. Swapping sandals for court shoes, pumps or loafers can also turn an outfit around. Make use of comfortable styles by reproducing them in various classic colours ... The options are endless.

Transform one basic garment by changing only the accessories.

For day wear, the little black dress can be worn with a loose sweater casually draped over the shoulders, thongs, a straw or raffia handbag and sunglasses. The accessories should be pale and soft in colour.

To transform the look for a cocktail party, the same dress can be worn with a chiffon scarf, sheer pantihose, stylish shoes, a small, sequined evening bag and diamanté earrings. Stick to one colour for evening elegance.

Carry a basic wardrobe through the seasons, summer to winter.

During the hot summer months, this simple, versatile straight skirt can be worn with a crisp cotton, short-sleeved shirt, patent loafers, a shoulder bag and sunglasses. Undo the top two buttons of the shirt for extra comfort.

Warm up for winter by adding a complementary jacket. Button up and wear a cherry-red woolly scarf to keep the cold wind at bay. You can use the same shoes and handbag, but add pantihose for extra warmth.

Clever Combinations

Convert corporate-casual to corporate-chic by changing textures.

For a casual appearance, wear loose weaves and knits with easy draping to complement elegant trousers. Wear the Pashmina shawl over one shoulder and complete the outfit with a rough-textured, informal shoulder bag.

Formalize the look by refining the textures. Wear the same trousers and top, but add a matching, fine-textured jacket to form a suit. Don a leather belt and handbag and drape the Pashmina shawl as indicated.

Modify the look by changing the structure of the silhouette.

This straight-legged trouser and lilac top reflects a casual appearance when worn with an unstructured, loose-knit sweater and strappy sandals. A simple black handbag completes the outfit.

To create a corporate look, all that is needed is to add a suitable structured jacket and exchange the casual sandals for closed, high-heeled court shoes. The same handbag can be used for both styles.

Clever Combinations

Adapt from corporate to cocktail at short notice by paring down.

Dress and jacket suits are elegant, smart and ideal for the workplace. Add a scarf, a long gold neckchain, court shoes, a slingbag and sunglasses, and you will be suitably prepared for any out-of-office meeting.

Caught unawares with no time to change before the cocktail party? Make small but creative changes by paring down the corporate look. Remove the jacket and scarf and use the neckchain as a waist chain for evening chic.

138

Change an outfit from casual to smart by using different tones.

The more tones of a single colour theme that are used in garments and accessories, the more casual the look appears. Compare this skirt, top, cardigan, jacket and shoes with the outfit alongside.

By simplifying and repeating the same tone throughout, a new, smarter look can be achieved with the existing garments. Wear a lighter-coloured top and shoes that tone in with the rest of the outfit.

Clever Combinations

Combine modern and traditional classics from home to a meeting.

For casual comfort while working from home, wear denim jeans, a white cotton T-shirt and lace-up shoes. Add a spotted red scarf tied at the waist for colour, and a navy blazer when feeling cold.

Simply exchange the modern T-shirt for a traditional white cotton shirt and transfer the scarf from the waist to the neck. Button up the navy blazer, grab your handbag and you're ready for that meeting.

Create new styles by colour blocking favourite shapes.

A working holiday wardrobe can be created with black, flat-front trousers, a red-and-white striped T-shirt and a white shirt worn as a jacket. Add a black scarf, thongs and a raffia handbag to complete the look.

Use the same styles in different colours with minor accessory changes to smarten up the look: red trousers, black T-shirt, the same white shirt tucked in, red-and-white scarf, black handbag and loafers.

Glossary

Baste Sew with loose, temporary stitches.

Breakpoint A point at the centre-front edge where the revers starts to fold back.

Ease An extra measurement that is added to ensure comfort or a looser fit.

Interfacing Usually very light fabric, which is sewn beneath the facing of a garment to provide shape and firmness.

Mitre A diagonal join of approximately 45 degrees where the hems along two sides meet at a corner.

Notch Symbols that are transferred from patterns to fabrics to indicate matching points.

Perpendicular A vertical line at a right angle to a horizontal line.

Placket A garment opening fastened with a zip, buttons or hooks and eyes.

Revers The lapel of a jacket or blouse which is an extension of the garment front edge.

Roll line The line from the breakpoint to the shoulder on which the revers folds.

'Stitch in the ditch' Stitch in the seam line to minimize time-consuming hand tacking.

Index

143